AH-1 Cobra
in action

By Wayne Mutza
Color by Don Greer
Illustrated by Ernesto Cumpian

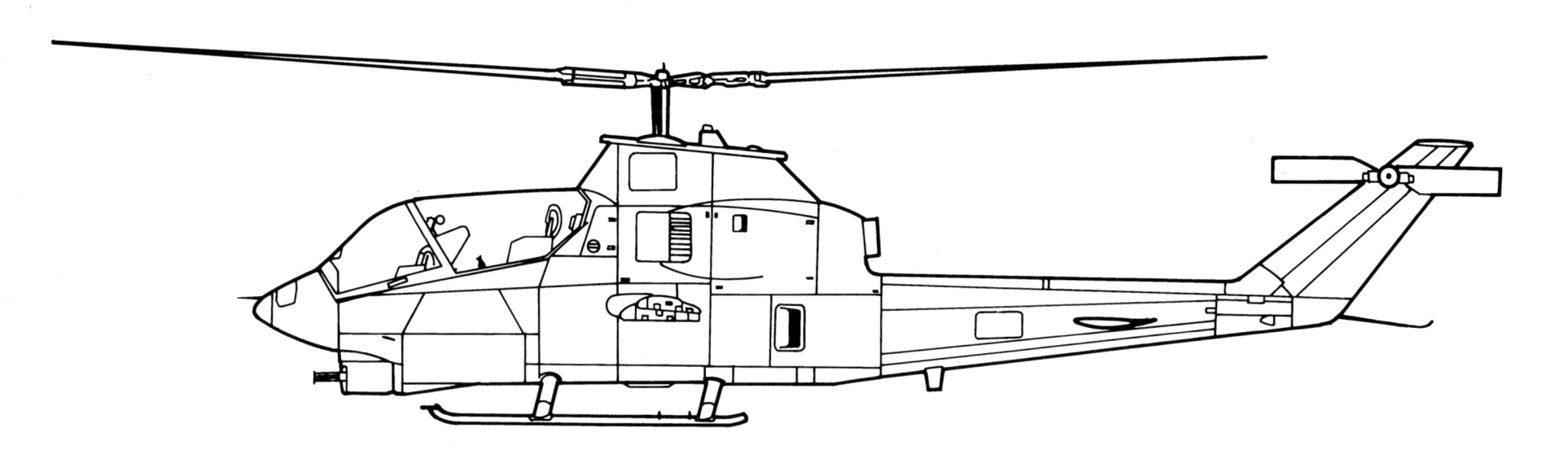

Aircraft Number 167
squadron/signal publications

AH-1Ws of HMLA-169 "Vipers" brings an Iraqi armor column under attack with TOW missiles during *OPERATION DESERT STORM*

Acknowledgements

This book would not have been possible without the kind and able assistance of Bob Leder, Bell Helicopter Textron, Inc.; Regina Burns, US Army Aviation Museum; Capt. Tammy Gross; Capt. Stephen Watkins; Ron Osburn; Anthony Salerno; Danny Crawford; Terry Love and Skip Robinson.

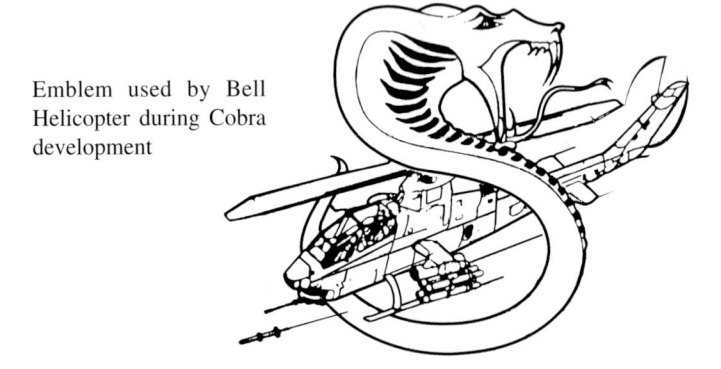

Emblem used by Bell Helicopter during Cobra development

Dedication

This book is dedicated to the United States Army Aviation Museum at Fort Rucker, Alabama whose exemplary efforts so well preserve the Army Aviation legacy.

COPYRIGHT 1998 SQUADRON/SIGNAL PUBLICATIONS, INC.
1115 CROWLEY DRIVE CARROLLTON, TEXAS 75011-5010
All rights reserved. No part of this publication may be reproduced, stored in a retrieval system or transmitted in any form by means electrical, mechanical or otherwise, without written permission of the publisher.

ISBN 0-89747-382-5

If you have any photographs of aircraft, armor, soldiers or ships of any nation, particularly wartime snapshots, why not share them with us and help make Squadron/Signal's books all the more interesting and complete in the future. Any photograph sent to us will be copied and the original returned. The donor will be fully credited for any photos used. Please send them to:

Squadron/Signal Publications, Inc.
1115 Crowley Drive
Carrollton, TX 75011-5010

Если у вас есть фотографии самолетов, вооружения, солдат или кораблей любой страны, особенно, снимки времен войны, поделитесь с нами и помогите сделать новые книги издательства Эскадрон/Сигнал ещё интереснее. Мы переснимем ваши фотографии и вернём оригиналы. Имена приславших снимки будут сопровождать все опубликованные фотографии. Пожалуйста, присылайте фотографии по адресу:

Squadron/Signal Publications, Inc.
1115 Crowley Drive
Carrollton, TX 75011-5010

軍用機、装甲車両、兵士、軍艦などの写真を所持しておられる方はいらっしゃいませんか？どの国のものでも結構です。作戦中に撮影されたものが特に良いのです。Squadron/Signal社の出版する刊行物において、このような写真は内容を一層充実し、興味深くすることができます。当方にお送り頂いた写真は、複写の後お返しいたします。出版物中に写真を使用した場合は、必ず提供者のお名前を明記させて頂きます。お写真は下記にご送付ください。

Squadron/Signal Publications, Inc.
1115 Crowley Drive
Carrollton, TX 75011-5010

(RIGHT) "**Your worst nightmare!**" The present day Cobra, the U.S. Marine AH-1W, is the most powerful and most versatile attack helicopter in the world, and the only type to feature a dual anti-armor capability. This Super Cobra is armed with "Hog" rocket pods, TOW missile launchers and Hellfire missiles.

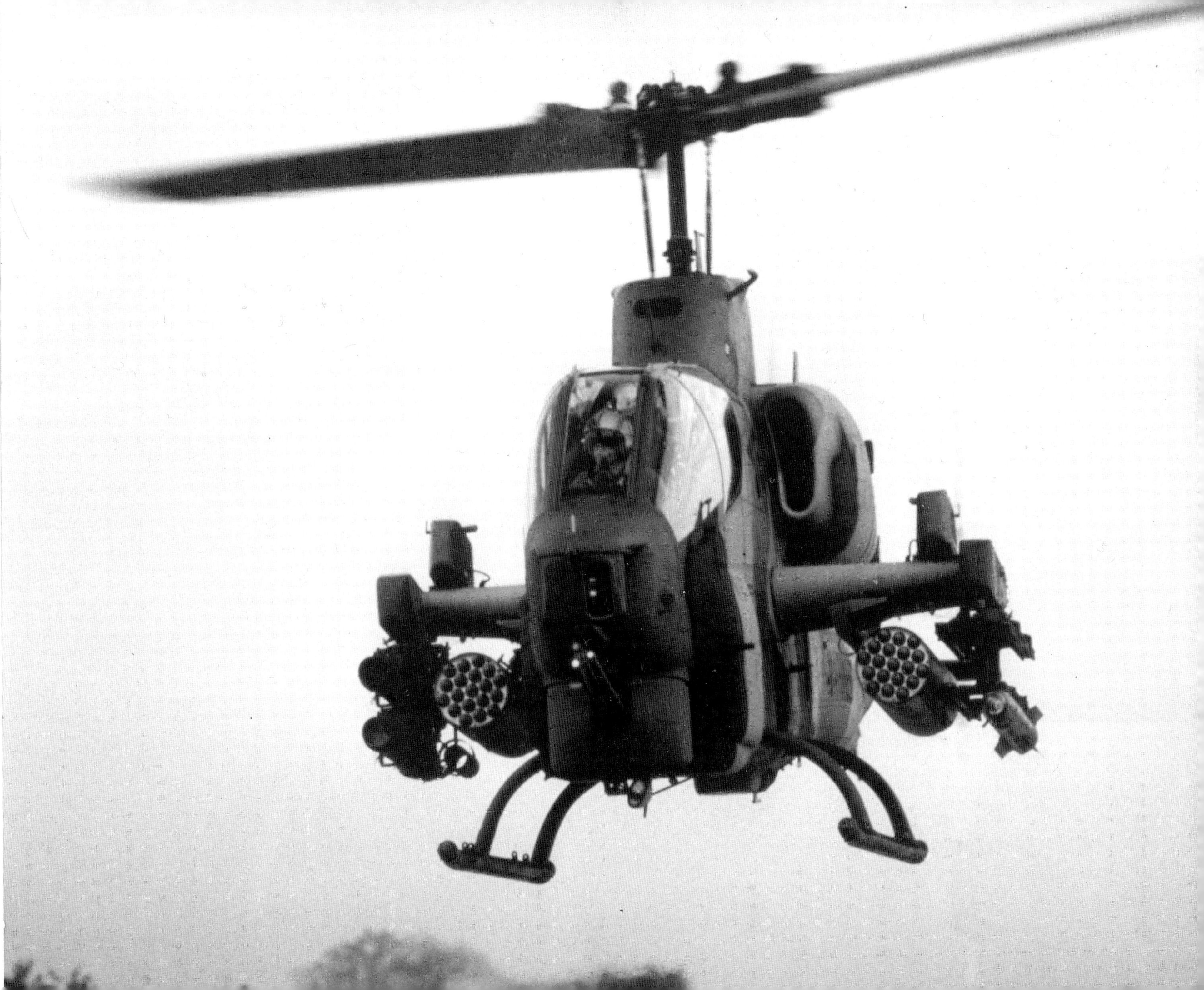

Introduction

The armed helicopter concept can be traced back to the early 1940s when Sikorsky began work on a bomb-dropping device for its R-4. Little came of the idea, or any other rotary-wing armament system, until a decade later, when the U.S. Army and the French shared the credit for the first armed helicopter. Their accomplishments went largely unnoticed until the Korean war, when the frequent unavailability of fixed-wing support, though superior, pointed out the need for heavily-armed helicopters to accompany transport helicopters. During the post-war period, the Army conducted, without official approval or support, extensive experimentation with a vast array of helicopter weapon systems, claiming they were operating (though rather loosely) under the directive to "test new concepts in mobility."

Nearly every helicopter in the Army's inventory underwent tests with weapon systems that ranged from crude makeshift devices to complex combinations of armament. However, soon after its debut, the Bell HU-1A (later UH-1A) Huey stood above the rest as the premier armed helicopter. When the UH-1A was deployed to Vietnam with rockets and machine guns during 1962, it became the first U.S. operational armed helicopter. Following close behind the A Model was the UH-1B featuring a more powerful engine and an increased weapons package. As the Army' standard gunship, the "Bravo" model was produced and used in large numbers.

The UH-lB's inability to keep up with faster Huey transports prompted the UH-1C, which was developed purely as a gunship. While it featured vast improvements over its predecessor, the "Charlie" model was an interim design pending what Army officials envisioned would be a true attack helicopter. Based on the UH-lB, the "C" model incorporated a more powerful engine, a semi-rigid 540 rotor system that substantially increased maneuvering, a cambered vertical fin for added directional stability, and an improved weapons package comprising rockets, miniguns and a 40mm grenade launcher nose turret.

Introduction of the faster UH-1 Huey and CH-47 Chinook transport helicopters forced Army officials to set their sights on the acquisition of a fully dedicated attack helicopter. In anticipation of battlefield requirements, Bell had prudently set to work on a much faster helicopter, with more firepower and maneuverability, which could be delivered in minimal time at low cost and without significant impact on the Army's established logistics and training structure.

During 1958, Bell had completed a narrow body helicopter gunship called the D245 Combat Reconnaissance Helicopter to coincide with the Army's experimental armed helicopter unit, the 7292nd Aerial Combat Reconnaissance Company. But with little priority given armed helicopter systems and no applicable doctrine, official support for the concept fizzled.

Undaunted, Bell continued to work, funding its own research, on a mock-up of an advanced weapons helicopter that made use of UH-l components. Labeled the D255 "Iroquois Warrior" and unveiled during June 1962, the new design incorporated tandem "stepped" seating for a pilot and gunner, mid-fuselage stub wings, a nose turret and a streamlined ventral gun pod. The D255's narrow fuselage was a revolutionary design that would become the trademark of future helicopter gunships. Not only did the slender profile present a smaller target to enemy gunners, but it offered nearly unlimited visibility for both crew members and excellent aerodynamic efficiency, which meant better handling characteristics and ordnance delivery. The Iroquois Warrior sparked Army interest to the degree that funding was allocated for research and development of an armed attack helicopter.

Bell received approval during December 1962 for the construction of a flying test bed, which turned out to be a significant deviation from the Iroquois Warrior. Derived from a combination of OH-13S and Model 47J-2 components to minimize costs, the Model 207 Sioux Scout was completed by August 1963. Impressed with the Model 207 after flight and weapons trials, the Army recommended the development of a similar aircraft, but with a turbine engine.

In the meantime, the Army announced its requirement for an Advanced Aerial Fire Support System (AAFSS), which prompted several manufacturers to begin work on sophisticated designs to meet the stringent requirements. The Lockheed AH-56 Cheyenne and Sikorsky's S-66 Blackhawk were chosen, however, the amount of time before production and delivery of the AAFSS, plus the pressing need for helicopter gunships in Vietnam, forced the Army to open a competition for an interim aircraft. Bell's entry, a trimmed version of the Iroquois Warrior called the D262, was eliminated.

Convinced that they could produce what the Army needed, Bell engineers decided in January 1965 to build a prototype incorporating well-proven components of the D262 and Sioux Scout. They, in turn, tried to convince the Army that the low lead time and low prototype development cost could result in quick deliveries for the Army inventory.

The Model 209 featured a narrow fuselage that accommodated a crew of two in vertically-tiered tandem seats, with the pilot above and behind the co-pilot/gunner. Ordnance hardpoints were attached to stub wings (which provided some lift) and an Emerson Electric chin turret housed a GAU-2B/A 7.62mm minigun. Power was supplied by a Lycoming 1,100shp T53-L-11 turbine engine, which drove a transmission and 540 rotor system of the UH-1C.

The Model D255 was Bell's first helicopter design to feature tandem seating for a pilot and gunner, stub wings and a nose turret. The slender ventral gun fairing, seen here on the "Iroquois Warrior", was not carried over to successive models. (Bell)

One early Cobra design featured long wings, the outboard halves of which lowered to form the aircraft's landing gear. (Bell)

The prototype made its first flight on 7 September. To conserve weight Bell's traditional stabilizer bar was replaced by a Stability Control Augmentation System (SCAS). On 25 October, it flew at a sustained speed of 200 mph, breaking the world speed record of 180.1 mph for a helicopter in its weight class.

As the war in Southeast Asia intensified, the Army was faced with a decision to either halt the AAFSS program, lower its requirements or select a suitable type for swift production. A compromise left the program in place while a competition was held to select an airframe that could be in production within 18 to 24 months. Of five entries, only Bell offered a new airframe with its Model 209. During a competition fly-off between the remaining entries at Edwards AFB during late November 1965, the Model 209 was favored over the Kaman UH-2 and Sikorsky S-61. Those results led to an Army contract for two prototypes on 4 April 1966. Nine days later, the Army ordered 100 production Model 209s.

To Bell employees, it was known simply as "Ship 1." Its initial designation of UH-1H went to the UH-1D's successor and the Model 209 became the AH-1G, which stood for "Attack Helicopter, Type 1, 7th in the Huey series." The name Cobra identified the Huey gun platoon of the 114th Aviation Company in Vietnam. A Bell representative visiting the unit liked the name and dubbed the 209 the Cobra on his return. Later, the U.S. Army adopted the official name of Huey Cobra at the suggestion of Army aviation pioneer General Hamilton H. Howze. Thus came the first deviation from the Army practice of naming aircraft after American Indian tribes or woodland animals.

By the mid 1970s, the Army implemented a modernization program to improve the performance, weapons, and survivability of its Cobra fleet. Successive improvements continued into the 1980s, which resulted in the AH-1Q and various forms of the AH-1S, which were later redesignated AH-1E, F and P. The last Army Cobras were delivered during 1986, with all four major configurations operational in the U.S., Germany and Korea in the 1990s. As the winner of the Army's Advanced Attack Helicopter competition held during the mid 1970s, the Apache was considered well beyond the AH-1's capabilities, a view not necessarily shared by the U.S. Marine Corps.

The Marine Corps, which had long resisted arming helicopters, quickly and dramatically realized the need to instantly suppress enemy ground fire in Vietnam, especially during the critical moments just before and after touch-down in a landing zone.

Impressed with the UH-1E Huey's performance as a gun platform, the Marines were convinced that the Huey's systems should be developed to the point where flight performance limitations were held to a bare minimum. The timely introduction of the Huey Cobra not only bolstered that concept, but ensured the AH-1 Cobra series a long career in the Marine inventory. By being integral to infantry units, Cobras adapted to the Marine's all-important "unity of command" principle, while closing the gap between fixed-wing attack and observation squadrons.

Long after the Army began phasing out Cobras in favor of the AH-64 Apache, the Marine Corps continued to refine the Cobra, firm in their belief that the type was best suited for their attack mission. Therefore, the AH-1 series was progressively developed to keep pace with Marine tactical requirements.

Shortly after the AH-1G had entered production, the Marines expressed their interest in a twin-engine version, citing the need for increased power and a broadened safety margin over water. Bell complied with the AH-lJ SeaCobra, whose success led to the AH-1T during the mid 1970s. During the early 1980s, the "Tango" was vastly improved when the Marine Corps decided to capitalize on the technology already present to modify their AH-1T. The result was the AH-lW SuperCobra, which became the most powerful and heaviest member of the Cobra family. Literally a flying arsenal, the "Whiskey" more than satisfied the Marine specifications for a lethal escort and close-support helicopter that could operate in any climate.

Already loaded with sophisticated weapons and electronics systems, the Marine Whiskey Cobra faces new technology up-grades in the early 2000s to take full advantage of the airframe's 20 year life span.

Only 36 inches wide, the first generation Cobra offered a very limited head-on target profile. This prototype had nose landing lights, a dummy turret and a hastily cut air intake on the rotor pylon. (Bell)

Wearing a red registration number for its European tour, the first Model 209 makes its debut at Le Bourget Airport during June 1967. Below the gold Cobra emblem on the tail fin is serial 47015. (Jack Friell)

Development

Model 207

AH-1G

AH-1S(MOD)

AH-1P

AH-1E

AH-1F

AH-1J

AH-1T

AH-1W

AH-1-4BW

AH-1G Cobra

The introduction of the AH-1G Cobra brought a number of changes from the Model 209. A 1,400 shaft horsepower (shp) T53-L-13 turbine engine replaced the 1,100shp L-11 which powered the Model 209. The Avco Lycoming L-13, which drove the 540 rotor system, supplied 200 more horsepower than the L-11.

When Bell engineers realized that the first aircraft's retractable skid landing gear was a weak compromise of less safety and added maintenance over a slight speed increase, fixed gear was ordered for the AH-1G. A ventral extension on the 209's tail fin, to enhance directional stability, was also deemed unnecessary and deleted from production plans. In addition, a switch was made to the larger diameter TAT-102A weapons turret to accept the XM-28 dual weapons system, then under development.

Two pre-production machines (often called YAH-1Gs) were ordered for the Army, which assigned them serial numbers 66-15246 and 15247. After completing its maiden flight on 15 October 1966, the first AH-1G underwent rigorous tests which included armament trials at Fort Hood, Texas. The second AH-1G flew for the first time on 10 March 1967 and was used primarily for Stability Control Augmentation System (SCAS) trials. It would later be used for the initial training of Vietnam-bound New Equipment Training Team (NETT) personnel. By the end of May, the first two production machines were rolled out and turned over to the Army in June.

The power plant and rotor system of the AH-1G gave it a cruise speed of 166 mph and a maximum dive speed of 220 mph. A 247-gallon fuel capacity allowed a range of 362 miles at an operating weight of 6,070 pounds. Maximum takeoff weight was 9,500 pounds and the service ceiling was 12,700 feet. The 540 rotor system incorporated a wide-chord main rotor which was 44 feet in diameter, and an 8 foot 6 inch diameter tail rotor. The overall height of the AH-1G was 13 feet 6 inches.

The original Cobra's basic construction set the standard for all subsequent models. Internal and contour beams combined with honeycomb panels created a sturdy airframe and left ample space outside the beams for various components, which were easily accessible through exterior panels. A honeycomb floor not only minimized vibration but absorbed armament recoil. The tail boom was a carry over from the UH-1C which featured a distinctive cambered fin.

In the interest of aerodynamic efficiency, all forward fuselage panels were flush-riveted and most antennas were installed flush or within the airframe. Post-1966 AH-lGs had the nose landing light relocated to a retractable type on the belly, immediately aft of the turret.

Based on combat experience with the UH-1 Huey, the Cobra's fuel tanks were made self-sealing and vital components, including the engine compressor, fuel control and hydraulic system, were shielded with armor plating. Crew protection took the form of a bulletproof windshield, an armored nose plate for the gunner and armored seats with sliding side panels.

Armament for the Cobra initially consisted of an Emerson Electric TAT-102A turret with a single GE XM-134 7.62mm minigun rated up to 4,000 rounds per minute (rpm). It was replaced during later production by an M28A1 sub-system, housed in a TAT-141 turret, which incorporated a GAU-2B/A mini-gun and an M-129 40mm grenade launcher, or two of each. Each minigun had a 4,000 round supply of ammunition and could fire at a rate of 2,000 or 4,000 rpm in six-second bursts. The grenade launcher fired at a rate of 450 rpm and carried a 231 round ammunition supply. Although normally operated by the gunner, the turret could be

The original Model 209 featured retractable landing gear and a ventral fin, both of which were later deemed unnecessary and deleted from successive models. (Bell)

The first three Cobras. The original Model 209 (foreground) is accompanied by the first two prototypes. The tail boom of Serial Number 66-15246 was checkered for camera tracking. (Bell)

Generals Howze and Westmoreland, along with Bell President Ducayet, are among the officials reviewing four notable Cobras during 1967. The original 209, wearing fresh camouflage, is flanked by the second prototype, the first of a large production batch 68-15000 and number 66-15248, a one-off test platform. (Bell)

The second prototype (66-15247), armed with a single mini-gun in the turret, undergoes armament tests at Ft Hood during 1967. Red bands were painted on the nose and rotor pylon. (Ron Osburn)

fired by the pilot in the fixed-forward position. Likewise, the gunner could fly the aircraft with "armchair" controls introduced in the 207 Scout.

The stub wings spanned 9 feet 4 inches and were stressed to carry a wide variety of ordnance on four hardpoints. Wing stores included various types of tube launchers with warheads that included general purpose (GP), high explosive (HE), white phosphorus (WP - "Willie Pete"), flechettes ("Nails"), marking smoke and practice loads.

Rocket systems comprised a 7-shot XM-157 pod, replaced in 1966 by an XM-158, which was longer and used exposed replaceable tubes. A 19-shot XM-159 pod was later replaced in favor of an XM-200 unit. Five separate models of 19 shot pods were available, which ranged from 83 to 99 inches in length and weighed empty between 79 and 132 pounds. All rocket pods were dubbed "Hog pods", and with the use of four on the wings stubs were called a "Heavy Hog" configuration. Rocket pods were initially paired with podded 1,500-round XM-18 SUU-11A/A mini-guns. When the dual weapon turret was introduced, four rocket pods became the favored wing load. An LAU-10/A four-tube pod was also available for firing 5 inch Zuni rockets, but was seldom used.

Added to the AH-1G's arsenal during late 1969 was the General Electric six-barrel 20mm M61A1 Vulcan cannon. Designated the XM-35 system, the port side inboard installation included streamlined fairings above the skids for ammunition storage, along with raised panels below the cockpit's port side to accommodate system wiring. Most XM-35-equipped AH-lGs filled out their armament load with outboard XM-158s and a starboard XM-18 system. Weapon loads and configurations were usually dependent upon targets expected, unit policy and personal preference. A total of 1,126 AH-lGs were produced, with the last example delivered during February 1973. Many would undergo extensive modification to extend their service lives.

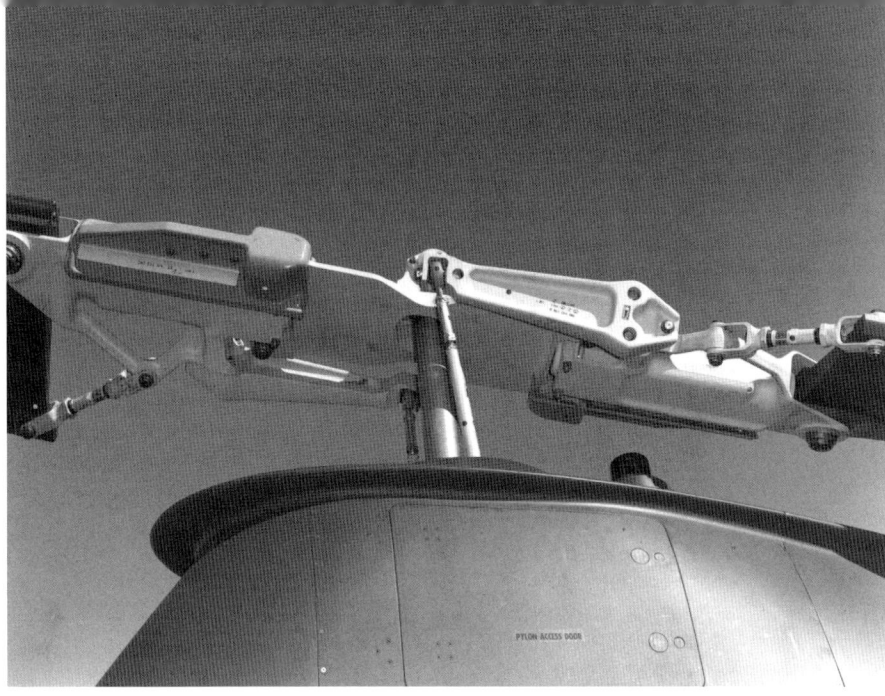

Bell's simple, but highly effective, 540 rotor system, which was also used on the AH-1G's predecessor, the UH-1C Huey gunship. (Bell)

The original Model 209 evaluated a 30mm turret during mid 1969. Besides an enlarged ammunition canister, the tan and green camouflaged Cobra has been fitted with dummy TOW missiles and an associated nose sighting unit. (Bell)

Cameras are mounted to the sixth-built AH-1G during armament tests. The 19-shot rocket pod has fore and aft fairings which were rarely in place during operational use. (Bell)

The hoses running over the seats and the rectangular air inlet at the base of the rotor pylon are part of the crew's air conditioner. Crews quickly discovered that the large sealed cockpits of early Cobras were intolerable solariums in warm climates. (Bell)

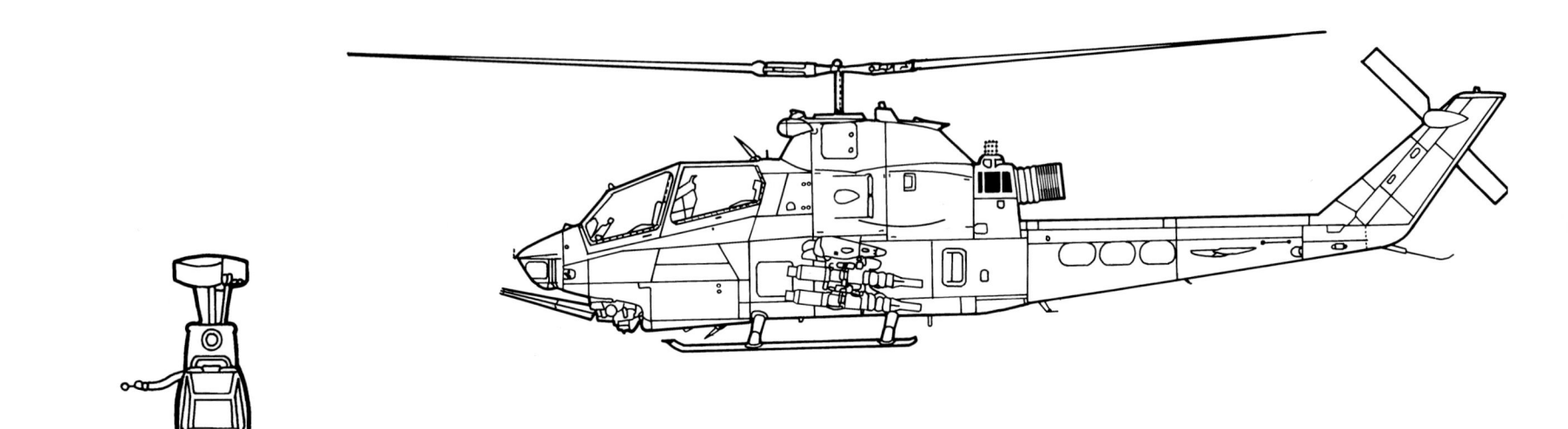

AH-1F Specifications

Length (Fuselage)	44 ft. 7 in.
Height	13 ft.
Main Rotor Diameter	44 ft
Tail Rotor Diameter	8 ft. 6 in.
Empty Weight	6,598 lbs.
Maximum Gross Weight	10,000 lbs
Armament	8 TOW Missiles
	20mm/30mm cannon
	70mm rockets and High Explosives, Multipurpose or smoke wing stores
Cruise Speed	155 mph
Service ceiling	12,400 feet
Range	300 nautical miles
Crew	2

Standard on all Cobra models were attachment points atop the skids for installation of ground handling wheels. (Author)

During the post-Vietnam war period, a number of AH-1Gs were painted unusual camouflage schemes. This Cobra of the 155th AHS wore a pattern of tan, dark gray and medium and dark green. The "Hog" rocket pods are equipped with breakaway nose fairings. (MAP)

Part of the batch of 38 AH-1Gs diverted to the U.S. Marines during a test flight in 1969. Marine AH-1Gs were painted Marine Field Green with white letters and numbers. (Bell)

Finished in glossy Marine Field Green, this AH-1G was assigned to the U.S. Navy Test Pilot School during 1975. Markings denoting assignment to HMA-773 have been taped over on the lower tail boom below "MARINES". The turret carries no weapons and a red instrument boom is attached to the nose. (Stetjger via Terry Love)

11

Vietnam

Prior to the delivery of AH-lGs to Army units, the Aviation Material Command eased the Cobra's introduction by forming the AH-1G New Equipment Training Team (NETT) on 1 August 1966. The NETT's two-fold mission was to completely learn the aircraft at Bell in order to teach future instructors and train the first Vietnam based AH-1G unit in-country.

Shortly after the first production AH-lGs were delivered to Army units, the NETT set up shop with six Cobras during August 1967 at Bien Hoa Air Base, South Vietnam. The first flight occurred on 31 August and four days later, exactly two years after the prototype was rolled out, the AH-1G received its baptism of fire. What began as a routine flight became a combat sortie when S/N 66-15263 joined Huey gunships engaging an enemy force near Can Tho in the Mekong Delta.

The 334th Assault Helicopter Company (AHC) in Vietnam had the distinction of being the first combat unit to operate Cobras. The unit's 1st Platoon "Playboys" began exchanging their UH-lC Hueys for Cobras during late September 1967 and on 8 October recorded the AH-1G's first official combat mission. Opening day was a success when two Playboy AH-lGs escorted ten troop-carrying Hueys of the 118th AHC during a combat assault, and later destroyed four enemy bunkers and fourteen sampans.

The Cobra's performance during the first year of combat in Vietnam was closely monitored by Bell. Very popular with Army aviators was the Cobra's high speed and slim profile, which made it extremely difficult for enemy gunners to track and hit. Used to firing at the slower, wider and less-armed Hueys, enemy troops were often reluctant to fire at the new Cobras.

With the new AH-1G came a whole new approach to helicopter gunship tactics. Increased maneuver, zero loading, and speed afforded a substantial increase in dive angle on a target while adding more variance to the target approach speed. Army helicopter pilots now possessed the ability to perform maneuvers previously limited to fixed-wing aircraft. Where UH-1 pilots would never even think of over-flying a target after a gun run, AH-1G pilots did so on a regular basis, relying on their speed and slender silhouette for safety.

Even with that the Cobra's increasingly proven record of safety and battlefield effectiveness, there were Army helicopter pilots who cited drawbacks to the AH-1G's combat effectiveness. Those who had become accustomed to, and relied heavily upon, the extra eyes, ears and firepower of two door gunners, found that the Cobra's soundproof cockpit made it extremely difficult to detect close ground fire. Huey door gunners could not only detect hostile fire, but were quite adept at laying down heavy volumes of suppressing fire to the sides, as well as below, the aircraft. In addition, many gunship pilots, even after amassing combat hours in Cobras, preferred the security and cohesiveness of door gunners. The door gunner-equipped Huey versus Cobra argument thrived in the gunship community throughout the war.

The enclosed cockpit also proved troublesome in hot climates. The ventilation air blowers installed in early AH-1G cockpits proved ineffective in Vietnam's oppressive heat. The solution was a small but powerful air conditioner called an Environmental Control Unit (ECU).

Throughout the conflict, the AH-1G served with Assault Helicopter Companies, Air Cavalry Troops, Aerial Weapons Companies and Aerial Rocket Artillery Batteries. Assault Helicopter Companies and Air Cavalry troops were similar in that they used Hueys for troop transport and a Cobra gun platoon for armed escort. Air cavalry units commonly paired AH-1Gs with OH-6A scout helicopters to form "hunter-killer" or "pink" teams. A two-Cobra section was called a "fire team", which became a "heavy fire team" with the addition of a third AH-1G. The three Cobra-equipped weapons platoons of an aerial weapons company were assigned the

Displayed at Ft Rucker, Alabama this AH-1G is equipped with a 19 shot rocket pod and raised panels below the cockpit to accommodate wiring for an XM-35 cannon system. (Author)

2.75 inch Rocket Launchers

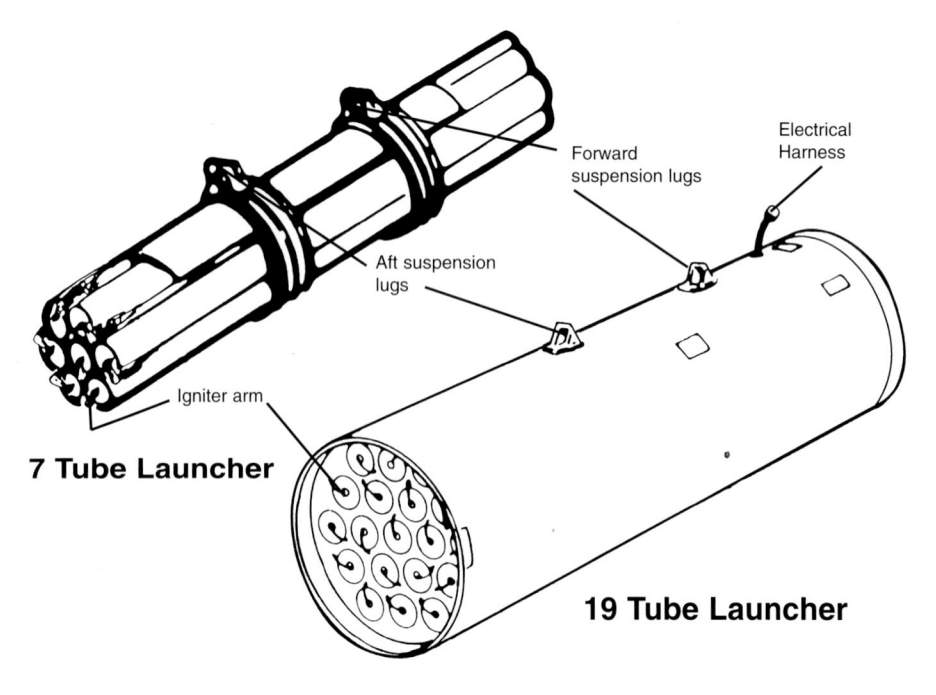

7 Tube Launcher

19 Tube Launcher

more liberal task of providing firepower on call. The aerial rocket artillery unit, with three Cobra platoons, was designed to deliver heavy rocket fire in support of troops operating beyond ground artillery range.

Cobras in Vietnam were not necessarily limited by their unit's basic mission. Armed reconnaissance, armed escort and close fire support was the Cobra's forte and, as such, was supplied to just about any that requested such. Cobra drivers were not beyond diverting from pure gunship status to rescue downed crewmen, who were picked up and flown out while perched precariously on open ammunition bay doors.

It wasn't until the TET offensive in early 1968 that the AH-1G was bloodied in a major campaign. Delivering close-in fire support, Cobras repelled major attacks on Saigon and Bien Hoa AB. Unlike fixed-wing aircraft that were corralled in their revetments by heavy incoming fire, the Cobras were able to quickly get airborne and unleash massive firepower with lethal accuracy.

The second major command in Vietnam to receive Cobras was the 1st Cavalry Division (Airmobile), which began operations with AH-1Gs during the Fall of 1968. As the number of Cobras deployed to Vietnam increased, the Cobra participated in everything from major offensives, such as the Cambodian incursion of May 1970, to small unit actions. The enemies' Spring offensive in 1972 set the stage for the first Cobra versus tank confrontation. The Cobra affirmed its status in the tank-killing business when one AH-1G unit alone destroyed or incapacitated more than 20 tanks, mostly with rockets. At the controls were crews of F Battery, 79th Aerial Field Artillery of the 1st Cavalry's 3rd Brigade.

During that action, AH-1Gs traded blows with intense enemy anti-aircraft fire, which included heat-seeking SA-7 surface-to-air (SAM) missiles. SAMs claimed two Cobras, prompting the Army to quickly modify the AH-1G's exhaust system. Early attempts to line the exhaust

The removable ammunition container for the XM-35 30mm cannon. Outboard of the cannon's mount is an XM-200 rocket pod. (Terry Love)

pipe with heat-reducing thermal elements proved ineffective and gave way to an upturned pipe that directed exhaust into the main rotor, thereby reducing the infra-red signature. The device was a compromise since it had a mildly adverse effect on performance and subsequent ordnance weight limits. To further counter the SAM threat, RCM ALQ-44 infra-red kits were added to AH-1Gs, as well as UH-1s. The unit was mounted atop the engine cowling, just forward of the exhaust.

Combat experience in Vietnam brought about additional modifications, foremost of which was the relocation of the tail rotor from the port to the starboard side. The switch was made to improve directional control, which had been adversely affected by the tall tail fin's sensitivity to tail winds. This modification, which was accomplished both at Bell and in the field in Vietnam, usually involved a tail boom replacement.

Changes in turret armament had the TAT-102, with a single minigun, replaced with an XM-28 mounting either two miniguns or one gun and a grenade launcher.

During the Vietnam conflict, Army AH-1Gs served with more than 20 combat units. As

7.62 mm M18A1 Gun Pod

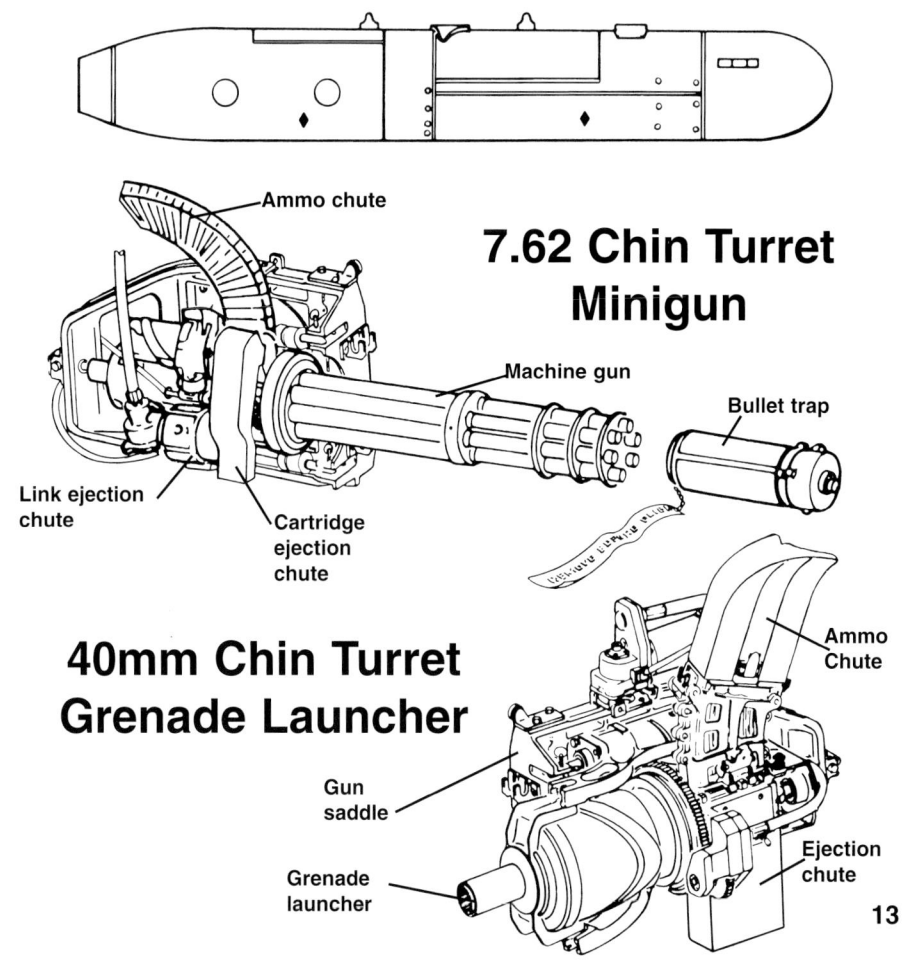

7.62 Chin Turret Minigun

40mm Chin Turret Grenade Launcher

13

An early AH-1G fires 2.75-inch rockets. The breakaway nose fairing can be seen tearing away from the launcher. (Bell)

This AH-1G has an XM-18 smoke dispenser attached to the bottom of the rocket pod. Capping the mini-gun is a lead-tipped bullet trap should the weapon be accidentally fired. (Bell)

testimony to the large number of AH-lGs committed to the war, in August 1968 there were 197 AH-lGs in-country and by year's end, just four months later, that number had already reached 337. Pending delivery of the twin-engine SeaCobra, 38 AH-1Gs were diverted to the Marine Corps as an interim measure during 1969. The first four machines became operational for combat evaluation with VMO-2, 1st Marine Air Wing (1st MAW) at Marble Mountain Air Facility near DaNang during early April. The first mission, a CH-46 med-evac escort, took place on 18 April. By December, VMO-2 had its full complement of 24 AH-lGs. While Marine use of the AH-1G paralleled that of the Army, VMO-2 added the role of armed observation, much like their OV-1OA Broncos. Marine AH-1Gs eventually took over many UH-1E Huey duties, freeing the war-weary Hueys for other vital missions and which was better suited to the type.

A reorganization of USMC helicopter units on 16 December 1969 resulted in the establishment of HML (Helicopter, Marine, Light) squadrons. The following December, VMO-2's assets were dispersed with UH-1Es being assigned to HML-167, while the AH-lGs formed HML-367.

The AH-lJ arrived in Vietnam on 18 February 1971, in time to participate in Lam Son 719, the massive South Vietnamese incursion into Laos, which lasted until April. The four AH-1J aircraft were assigned to HML-367 for a two-month combat evaluation period. Four days after their arrival, the AH-1Js began a busy schedule of escorting CH-53 transports.

The Sea Cobra's armament package in Vietnam was one of two configurations, depending on the anticipated target. A "light" load (1,475 lbs) comprised maximum 20mm ammunition, 14 rockets and either forward-firing gun pods or other light ordnance. The "heavy" arrangement (2,400 lbs) consisted of 76 rockets and 300 rounds of 20mm ammunition. As a safeguard,

The pilot's (rear) cockpit of the Army AH-1G. (Bell)

The AH-1G gunner's XM-28 turret sighting station. The gunner could fly the aircraft with "armchair" controls; the throttle/collective is on the port and the cyclic is on the starboard. (Bell)

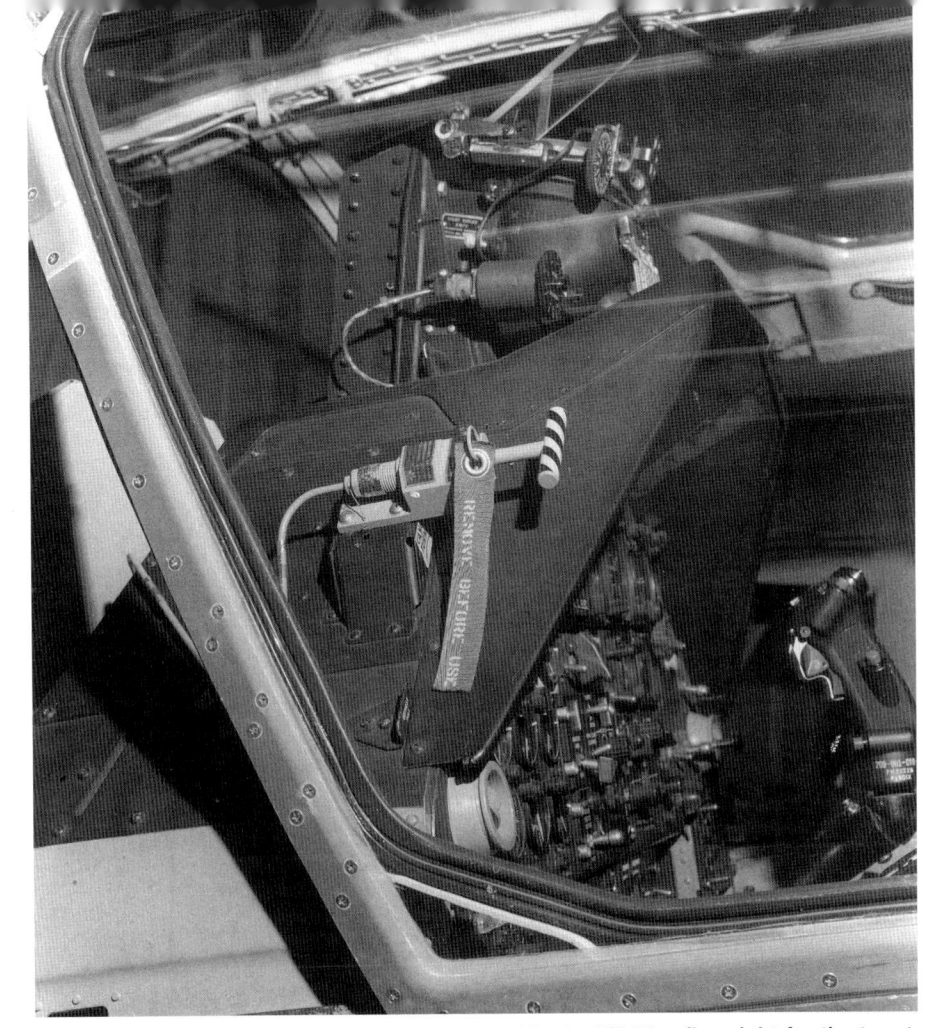

(Left) Mounted atop the pilot's instrument panel is the XM-73 reflex sight for the turret. The striped "T" handle activated the canopy removal mechanism. (Bell)

(Above) Some of the AH-1Gs assigned to the NETT were experimentally camouflaged in tan and green, however, Army commanders ruled against the scheme. Serial number 66-15259 carries the name "Virginia Rose I" under the cockpit. (Bell)

(Below) IRON BUTTERFLY was flown by A Troop, 1st Squadron, 9th Cavalry, 1st Cavalry Division in Vietnam during 1969. (George Sullivan)

AH-lJs and AH-lGs usually worked in pairs on missions, which usually entailed escorting heavy lift operations.

At the end of their successful evaluation, the AH-1Js were shipped from Vietnam, however, the type was re-deployed during the North Vietnamese offensive of 1972. Drawing the assignment was a Sea Cobra detachment of HMA-369 at MCAS Futema, Okinawa. The unit deployed aboard the USS DENVER (LPD-9) on 20 June and later flew from the USS CLEVELAND (LPD-7) and USS DUBUQUE (LPD-8). The Sea Cobras were used mainly to interdict vessels along the coast as part of the U.S. naval blockade and performed the FAC (Forward Air Controller) role for carrier aircraft. The AH-lJs returned to Okinawa when operations ceased on 18 January 1973.

Undoubtedly, the war in Southeast Asia was directly responsible for the development of the attack helicopter. The Army and Marines, despite initial reservations, found the Cobra ideal for the attack mission. The Cobra's exceptional accomplishments, however, were tempered by the loss of nearly 300 Army AH-1Gs, with one third of that number attributed to operational, or non-combat, losses. A total of 10 USMC Cobras were lost.

Army aviation units in Vietnam used geometric symbols for quick recognition by ground troops and other aircraft. The tiger in the diamond on this AH-1G identifies it as belonging to D Troop, 229th Assault Helicopter Battalion in 1969. An XM-200 rocket pod is mounted outboard while an XM-18 mini-gun pod occupies the inboard station. (George Sullivan)

Wearing its call sign SPUR 35 below the cockpit, this 20mm Vulcan cannon equipped AH-1G was stationed at Quan Loi in 1971. (Tom Hansen)

A crew chief poses with his AH-1G, distinguished as an early model by the nose landing lights and single-weapon turret. Inboard of the "Hog" rocket pods are XM-18 podded miniguns, which crews found much more reliable than the turret minigun. (Ron Osburn)

This was one of approximately 200 Cobras lost during combat action in Vietnam. The 1st Cavalry Cobra crashed during its attempt to land at its home base Lai Khe, after enemy gunners scored hits on the aircraft's fuel cell. (Mike Sloniker)

16

AH-1J SeaCobra

Having closely watched the Army's Cobra program and being assured of the Cobra's initial success, the Marine Corps considered the feasibility of a twin-engine Cobra variant to broaden the safety margin during over-water operations. However, due to budget restrictions the new Cobras were to be single-engine machines. That would change as a result of Marine UH-1E involvement, and subsequent losses during the "Tet" offensive in Vietnam during 1968, by giving the Marine Corps the leverage it needed to obtain the twin engine Cobra. The Marines also preferred a heavier armament package for the turret. Bell agreed with the concept and began work on the AH-1J during 1968. After it secured 38 Army-contracted AH-lGs to replace UH-1E losses in Vietnam, the Marine Corps ordered 49 AH-lJs during May of 1968. The first machine (157757) was rolled out on 14 October 1969 and made its first flight the following month.

A Pratt & Whitney Canada PT6T-4 Twin Pac engine (military designation T400-CP-400) used two turboshafts to drive a combining gearbox with a single output shaft. That gave the AH-1J, minus armament on the stub wings, a maximum speed of 175 mph at sea level and the ability to climb, on one engine, at 800 feet per minute. A rotor brake was added for shipboard operations and Navy avionics were installed.

Since the AH-1J differed considerably from the proven AH-1G, an intense evaluation was necessary prior to operational use. The first four examples went to NAS Patuxent River for Bureau of Inspection and Survey (BIS) trials during July 1970 which continued until March 1971. The next seven entered service with VMO-1 at MCAS New River during September for crew training. Four SeaCobras were attached to HML-367 in Vietnam for evaluation during early 1971. On 7 April 1971, five AH-lJs arrived at MCAS New River to form the first of four helicopter attack squadrons (one reserve). By the end of June, HMA-269 received 23 additional SeaCobras, making it the first fully equipped. It was followed later that year by HMA-169.

The AH-1J was slightly larger than the AH-1G and its tail fin was reinforced to handle the stress loads of an improved, wide-chord tail rotor. The liberal use of aluminum in the AH-1J's airframe enabled it to better withstand operations in corrosive salt-water environments.

The AH-1J introduced the Model XM-197 chin turret equipped with a three-barrel 20mm cannon with a 750-round capacity. Much like its predecessor, the AH-1J had four underwing stores stations for SUU-11A miniguns (inboard only) and various types of 2.75-inch rocket pods. A smoke grenade dispenser could be carried on the outboard wing station and AN/ALE-39 chaff dispensers were later mounted atop the wings. Eventually, the Marine AH-1J armament package was expanded to include MK-115 bombs, CBU-55 fuel-air explosives and AGM-114 Hellfire missiles.

In view of a Soviet helicopter gunship threat perceived during the early 1970s, it was decided that the SeaCobra should have air-to-air capability. Consequently, the Marines sought compatibility with the proven AIM-9 Sidewinder missile with the AH-1J and subsequent AH-1T. Bell proposed several installations and began test firings during 1984 with the AIM-9L launched from above and below the stub wings. While the AH-1J was slated for the Sidewinder installation, the Sidewinder only became operational on the AH-1T.

The AH-1J had a basic weight of 9,300 pounds and with a heavy combat load (turret plus four 19-shot rocket pods) weighed in at nearly 10,000 pounds, its maximum takeoff weight. A 270-gallon fuel capacity gave the SeaCobra a range of 288 nautical miles, which was drastically reduced to 120 miles with a heavy combat load.

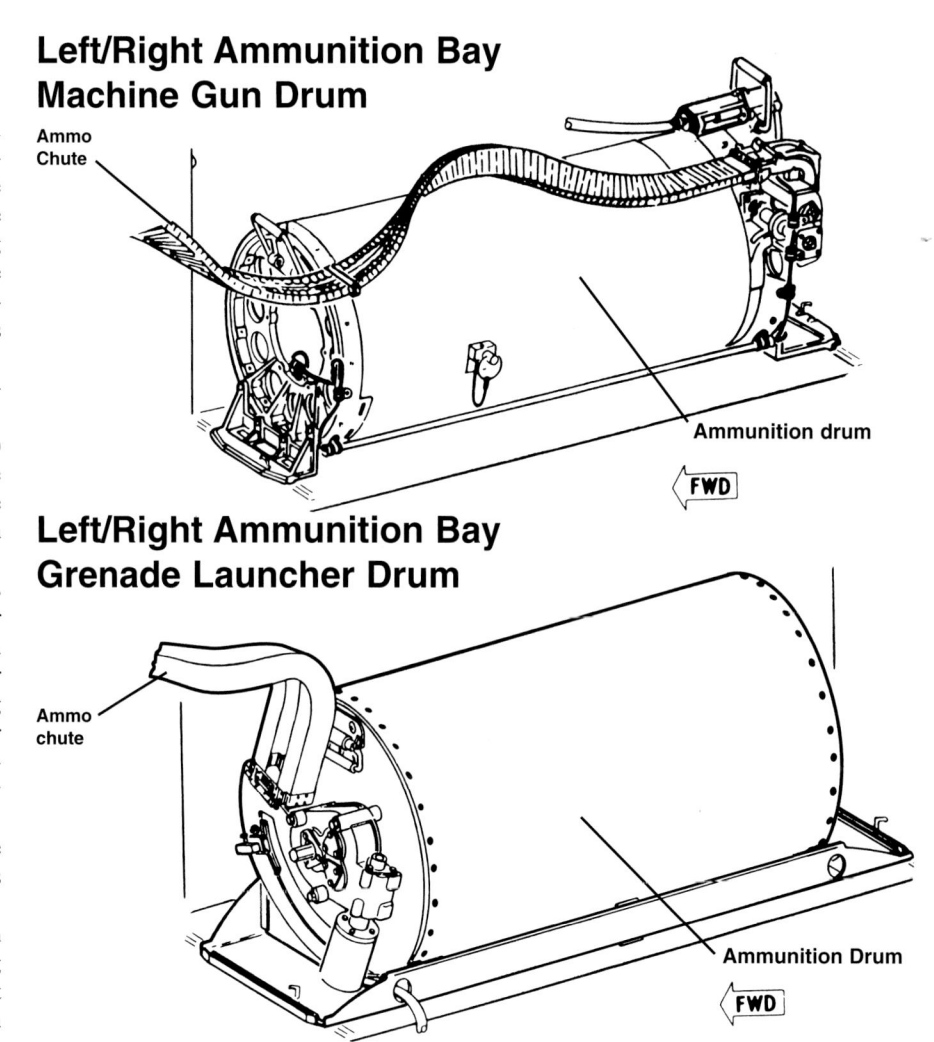

Left/Right Ammunition Bay Machine Gun Drum

Left/Right Ammunition Bay Grenade Launcher Drum

The first AH-1J built for the U.S. Marine Corps. (Bell)

A second contract brought the total procurement to 69 AH-1Js, the last of which left the assembly line during February 1975. A total of 202 AH-1Js, referred to as the "'International AH-1J", were exported to the government of Iran, 62 of which were TOW-equipped. Iran's AH-1Js were distinguished from USMC models by a larger diameter main rotor, a repositioned tail rotor and 1,970shp T400-WV-402 engines.

As a substantial improvement over the AH-1G in combat power and reliability, the AH-1J established a permanent place in Marine aviation for the attack helicopter and paved the way for continued development of the type.

(Right) Fitted with test instruments and wearing a red "2" on the front of its rotor pylon, the second-built SeaCobra during evaluation of the "heavy" armament load consisting of four 19-shot rocket pods. (Bell)

(Below) The fourth AH-1J lifts off from the tight quarters of a ship's fantail during sea trials. (Bell)

(Below) Mounted on the wing of this AH-1J is a "Redeye" missile launcher. The two-tube weapon was fired several times from the aircraft, but never qualified for operational use. Seen to good effect are the side bulges accommodating the SeaCobra's twin engine arrangement. (Bell)

Ground crewmen making a "Hot" re-arm (rotors turning) on a Cobra in Vietnam with 2.75-inch rockets. The AH-1G is armed with an XM-35 cannon and turret containing a mini-gun and grenade launcher. (Bell)

A trio of shark-mouthed Cobras headed for trouble over Vietnam's countryside. (Bell)

With nearly all of its major access panels open, an AH-1G of the 5th Aviation Detachment undergoes a 100-hour inspection at Vung Tau during September 1970. (us Army)

Although a large number of Cobras in Vietnam wore shark mouths, the design itself varied from one unit to another. Serial number 67-15455, of the 1st Squadron, 7th Cavalry, was one of the last AH-IGs produced with nose landing lights. (Bell)

This AH-1J mounts a movie camera on its wing during armament tests. (AAHS/Stephen Miller)

Wearing a two-tone sand camouflage, Bureau Number 157788 was a Bell demonstrator from the first production batch of AH-1Js. Accompanying the SeaCobra on its test flight is a Bell Model 214. (Bell)

Included among the subdued gray camouflage and markings of this AH-1J of HMLA-775 was the ever popular shark mouth. (Bob Shane via Terry Love)

Carrying a glossy dark green finish and high visibility markings during 1977, this AH-1J of HMA-169 represented a brief period after the Vietnam war prior to the introduction of subdued tactical paint schemes for Navy and Marine aircraft. (John Wegg)

KingCobra

Aware of the massive amount of Warsaw Pact armor in Europe, Bell Helicopter, in a move to dominate the gunship business, created a design for the anti-tank mission in mid-intensity conflict with enhanced survivability. Developed in secret, the Model 30 KingCobra expanded the AH-1G/AH-1J concept with emphasis on night capability. The innovative company-funded project took advantage of production hardware and proven systems. Although Bell targeted the Marines for use more than the Army, it was hoped that the KingCobra would edge out Lockheed's Cheyenne and Sikorsky's Blackhawk. Two prototypes were built: one powered by the Pratt & Whitney T400-CP-400 "Twin Pac", the same used in the SeaCobra, and another with a Lycoming T55-L7C rated at 2,850shp.

The fuselage of the KingCobra differed from its predecessor in that it was lengthened by four feet, strengthened for increased rotor thrust and gross weight, had a ventral fin and featured a modified nose and a larger ammunition bay. The stub wings were stretched to a span of 13 feet to carry more armament and fuel. A larger diameter 48 foot rotor had wider chord blades and double-swept tips to reduce noise and improve high-speed performance. The tail rotor diameter was increased to just over ten feet. At a gross weight of 14,000 pounds, the KingCobra had an endurance of more than three hours.

The Model 309's sophisticated systems included an ECM pod, radar warning, inertial navigator, APN-198 radar altimeter, Low Light Level Television (LLLTV), Forward Looking Infrared (FLIR) and helmet sights. A multi-sensor fire control system allowed day and night ordnance delivery.

Four hardpoints could accommodate 16 TOW missiles or a combination of weaponry that included rocket pods and anti-radar missiles. A GE turret contained a three-barrel 20mm gun with 1,345 rounds of ammunition, but could also accept a 30mm cannon and 1,000 rounds.

Construction of the pair began during January 1971 with the twin-powered prototype rolled out on 1 September 1971. Its first flight was accomplished on 10 September and exceeded 230 mph in a dive and performed three-G maneuvers during the first five hours of test flights. The

The single-engine Model 309 (foreground) crashed during April 1972, while the twin-engine version led to the development of the Marine AH-1T. Camouflage colors were medium and dark green. (Bell)

single-engine KingCobra was rolled out on 1 November, but crashed on 11 April 1972. In order to have a single-engine prototype available for Army evaluation, should the AH-56 Cheyenne program be canceled, Bell temporarily converted the first KingCobra to a single engine configuration.

Although the KingCobra never went into production, having been rejected by the Army, a 1974 Navy evaluation of the twin-engine prototype led to production of the Marine AH-1T.

The KingCobra was not only much larger than the original Huey Cobra, but its "TwinPac" powerplant drove a larger rotor system with swept tips. The modified nose incorporated a multi-sensor sight and an ammunition bay for linkless rounds. The streamlined fairing on the belly accommodated ammunition for the cannon. (Bell)

AH-1Q

Faced with a requirement to counter the threat posed by the Warsaw Pact's growing armor inventory during the early 1970s, the U.S. Army decided to convert half of its Cobra fleet to tank killers. Concurrently, Bell used the wealth of experience it gained with its pair of KingCobras to establish the Improved Cobra Armament Program (ICAP), which focused on integration of the TOW system into the AH-1G. Designated YAH-lQs, eight aircraft were developed under ICAP, the first of which was delivered to the Army during February 1973, with the last completed during July 1974.

Bell received a U.S. Army contract to modify 101 AH-1Gs with Hughes XM56 missile systems using XM128 helmet-mounted sights. An additional 189 AH-1Qs had been ordered by the end of 1974. The AH-1Q retained the original chin turret along with rocket pods on the inboard stations, while a four-round TOW launcher occupied each outboard station.

The original ICAP plan called for the conversion of 290 aircraft by August 1977, however, the TOW's additional 500 pounds adversely affected the Cobra's performance to the point that changes became necessary. To overcome the AH-1Q's weak performance during nap-of-the-earth (NOE) maneuvers, improvements were proposed which included airframe strengthening, a beefed-up drive train and most significant, an up-rated engine. The Improved Cobra Agility and Maneuverability (ICAM) program was established, which initially called for two aircraft as development platforms.

The "Q" Model gave the Army an attack helicopter that could operate in a mid-intensity environment. It would be the first derivative of the original Cobra modernized through a multi-phased program that added new features at each step.

With a camera mounted onto the right forward skid, an early AH-1Q undergoes TOW missile tests at Bell's Arlington facility. The gunner can be seen tracking the missile during its flight to the target. (Bell)

The AH-1Q, derived basically from an integration of TOW with the AH-1G, was the first deviation from the original Huey Cobra. The TOW system's Telescopic Sighting Unit (TSU) installation required that the pitot tube be relocated to the rotor pylon. Serial number 70-16055 was the first AH-1G converted to "Q" standards. (Bell)

TOW Missile Launcher

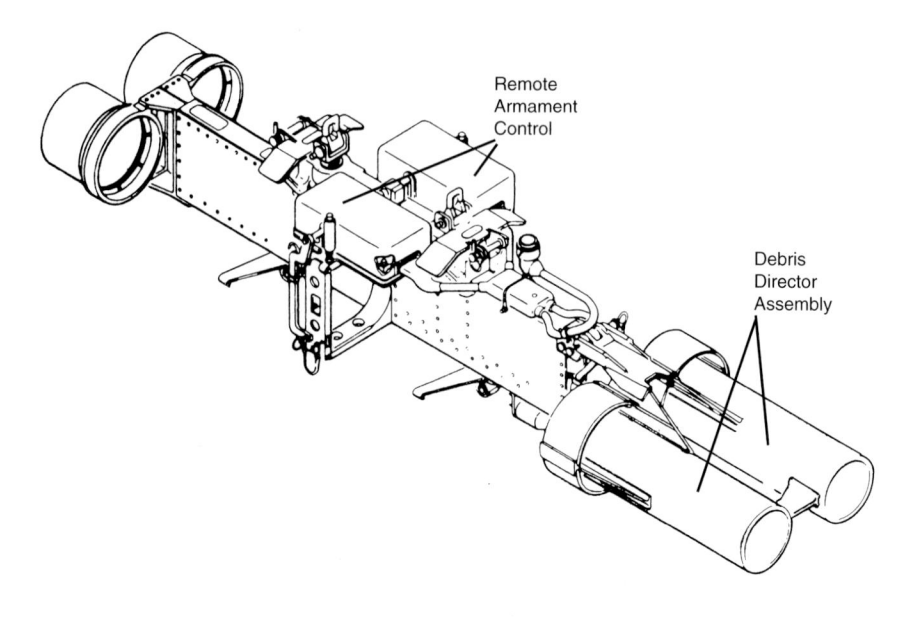

YAH-1R

One of the two AH-1Gs assigned to the ICAM program was serial number 70-15936. Designated YAH-1R, this Cobra served as a test bed without the TOW system, while the second machine assigned, a YAH-1Q redesignated YAH-1S, was TOW-equipped. Installation of a T53-L-703 engine in both aircraft provided an additional 400 horsepower, which boosted the maximum gross weight to 10,000 pounds. The YAH-1R and YAH-1S also received transmissions and tail rotor systems then in use in the AH-1J. Both machines were completed during December 1974 when they were turned over to the Army for tests. The YAH-1R was later used to evaluate modified rotor heads and composite blades and was eventually brought up to AH-1S standards.

AH-1S (MOD, PROD/P, ECAS/E, MC/F)

The third major step in the Cobra's continuing modification program had as its progenitor the YAH-1S, which was a AH-1Q converted as part of the ICAM program. During 1975, all AH-1Qs brought up to ICAM standards were designated AH-1S Modified (MOD), the first of four sub-variants. The balance of the original 290 AH-1Gs earmarked for conversion were delivered as AH-1S(MOD)s in full ICAM standards by March 1979.

Besides the switch made to the 1,800shp engine, a noteworthy improvement in the Cobra line were composite fiberglass main rotor blades. Most unusual was the fact that Kaman Aerospace Corp, under government guidelines directing that a portion of the major components be subcontracted, was awarded the contract to produce the new blades.

The majority of the converted Cobras were quickly deployed to Europe to help form a new attack helicopter force. By the end of 1977, the TOW Cobra fleet comprised 230 aircraft, with the remaining aircraft being dispersed among Ft Rucker and the 6th Cavalry Brigade at Ft Hood, Texas. On 2 May 1978, a contract was awarded to Dornier Reparaturwerft GMBH in Germany to convert 62 Germany-based AH-1Qs to AH-1S(MOD) standards. The last AH-1Q in the Army inventory was converted during February 1979.

Continuing development of the Cobra led to a contract for 100 new-construction aircraft designated AH-1S Production (PROD). This variant introduced a completely revised cockpit to enhance NOE operations and an IR signature suppressor. The AH-1S(PROD) retained the M-28 chin turret but incorporated the changes pioneered by the AH-1S(MOD). A new navigation package was installed along with smaller and lighter avionics equipment. This variant also introduced a seven-piece flat plate canopy, which reduced radar signature and reflectivity. A ballistic jettison system was incorporated into the new canopy.

The first AH-1S(PROD) (76-22567) was turned over to the Army on 16 March 1977 with deliveries being completed by August 1978. During March 1987, the AH-1S(PROD) was redesignated the AH-1P.

Of the original procurement order for 297 anti-armor production Cobras, the 101st machine (77-22763) was the first of 98 built as the AH-1S Enhanced Cobra Armament System (ECAS), also known as the "Up-Gun" Cobra. Redesignated the AH-1E during March 1987, this variant was basically an AH-1P with the M197 triple-barreled 20mm cannon turret added, a new SCAS rocket management systems provision, a 10 KVA alternator, and composite main rotor blades, which were distinguished by their tapered tips. The AH-1Es were delivered to the U.S. Army between September 1978 and October 1979.

The last group of improved production Cobras, starting with the 199th aircraft, became the

The Single YAH-1R while undergoing cold weather tests during March 1974. (Bell)

ultimate of the Army Cobra line. Two former AH-1Ps (76-22567 and 22600) were completed as prototypes for the AH-1S Modernized Cobra (MC), which became the AH-1F during March 1987. The pair began evaluation with the Army during July 1979, with the first AH-1F (78-23093) being delivered during November.

The "F" Model incorporated a number of technological advances over its predecessors. Its major improvements included a cockpit heads-up display (HUD), new rocket management system, fire-control computer, more efficient IR suppressor, AN/ALQ 144 IR jammer and a low airspeed data system. A laser range finder, doppler navigation system, APX-100 transponder and closed-circuit refueling were also added. An airborne laser tracker, located at the rotor pylon's leading edge, not only searches for, locks onto and tracks targets, but displays the data on the HUD and cues the TSU to the target.

By March 1981, Bell had delivered 99 AH-1Fs. During the early 1980s, the Army contracted for an additional 50 AH-1Fs for the National Guard. Deliveries began during April 1981 and 378 AH-1Gs were converted to "F" standards during 1982, bringing the total number of the type to 529. The last U.S. Army production contract was awarded in 1983 for 11 AH-1Fs. When the last Cobra delivery was made during 1986, the U.S. Army Cobra inventory reached nearly 1,100 aircraft.

During March 1987, the AH-1S(MOD) became known simply as AH-1S. Besides the T53-L-703 power plant, composite rotor blades, a wire strike protection system and AN/APR-39 radar warning became standard on all AH-1S variants. Despite vast improvements made in the AH-1S, dimensions changed little from the original Cobra. Today's Army Cobra is 44 feet, 7 inches in length with a height of 12 feet. The fuselage has retained its slender 3-foot width and all have a maximum gross weight of 10,000 pounds.

The AH-1F is currently undergoing a significant upgrade, giving Cobra a complete day-night capability. The U.S. Army is equipping many of its AH-1Fs with Hughes Cobra-Nite (C-Nite) targeting systems. C-Nite allows the Cobra to fire and track TOW missiles in day or night, through smoke, dust and adverse weather, while maintaining a countermeasure posture. Successful C-Nite system testing was conducted during late 1986 and early 1987, followed by Army purchases to keep their Cobra fleet combat effective beyond the year 2000. Although the venerable Cobras were being replaced in favor of AH-64 Apaches, the Army continued its evaluation of an air-to-air capability for its Cobras, along with a replacement for the L-703 engine.

As of this writing, all four AH-1S configurations are in service, with many overseas in Germany and South Korea, plus those flown by the Army National Guard in nearly 20 states.

A noteworthy AH-1S spin-off was the four-bladed PAH-2, on which the turret is replaced by a TADS/PNVS mission package. Besides an array of sophisticated systems, the PAH-2 can carry eight HOT missiles. Intended as a proposal for export, the type did not go beyond the design stage.

(Above) The AH-1S Telescopic Sight Unit and 20mm rotary cannon. Mounted at the center of the TSU is a wire deflector. (Terry Love)

(Left) The AH-1S(MOD) retained the original Cobra curved canopy design. The starboard panel accessed the pilot's compartment, while the front panel on the port side was used by the gunner. Below the cockpit was the ammunition bay, seen in its door open. (Author)

The AH-1S transmission installation. (Author)

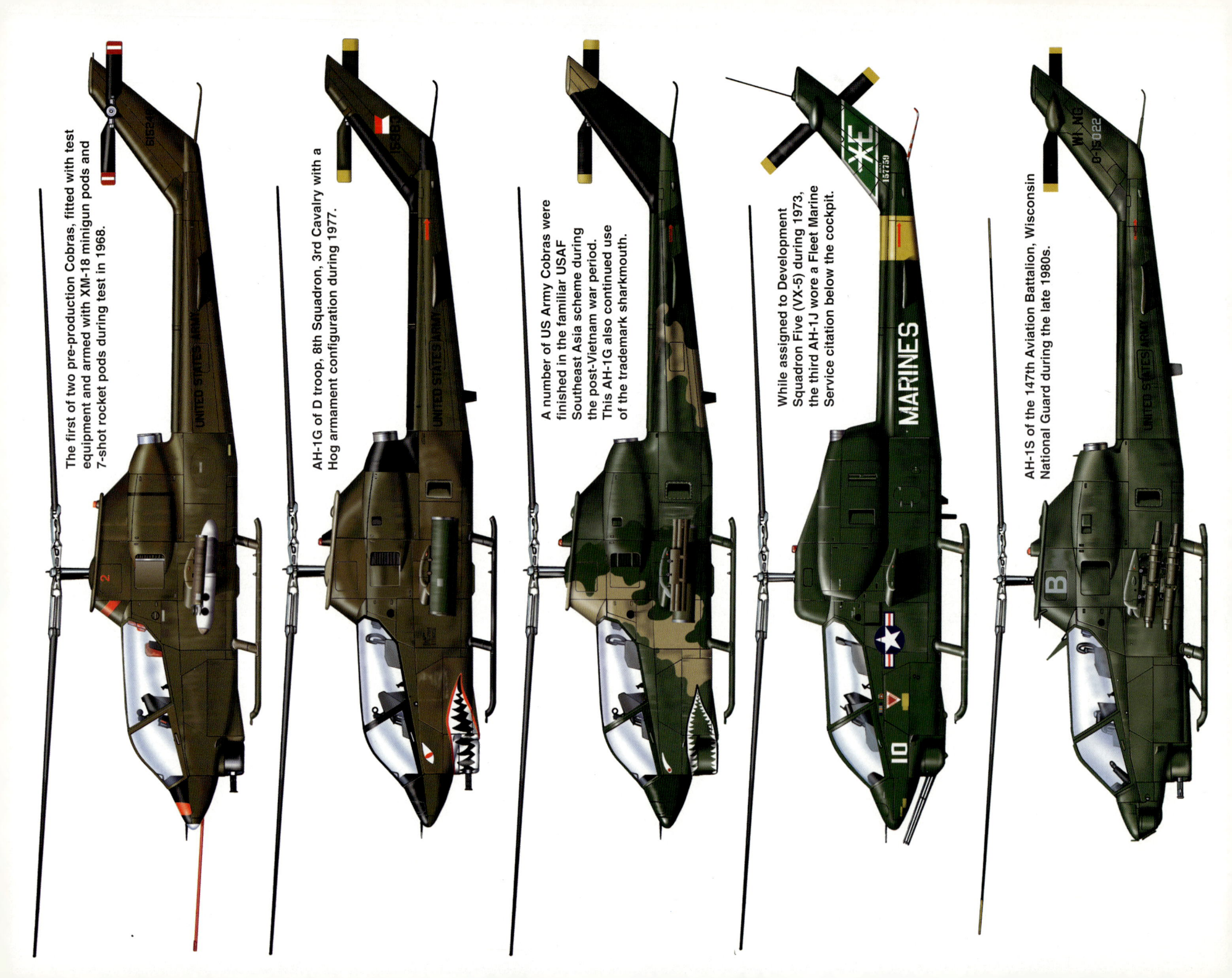

The first of two pre-production Cobras, fitted with test equipment and armed with XM-18 minigun pods and 7-shot rocket pods during test in 1968.

AH-1G of D troop, 8th Squadron, 3rd Cavalry with a Hog armament configuration during 1977.

A number of US Army Cobras were finished in the familiar USAF Southeast Asia scheme during the post-Vietnam war period. This AH-1G also continued use of the trademark sharkmouth.

While assigned to Development Squadron Five (VX-5) during 1973, the third AH-1J wore a Fleet Marine Service citation below the cockpit.

AH-1S of the 147th Aviation Battalion, Wisconsin National Guard during the late 1980s.

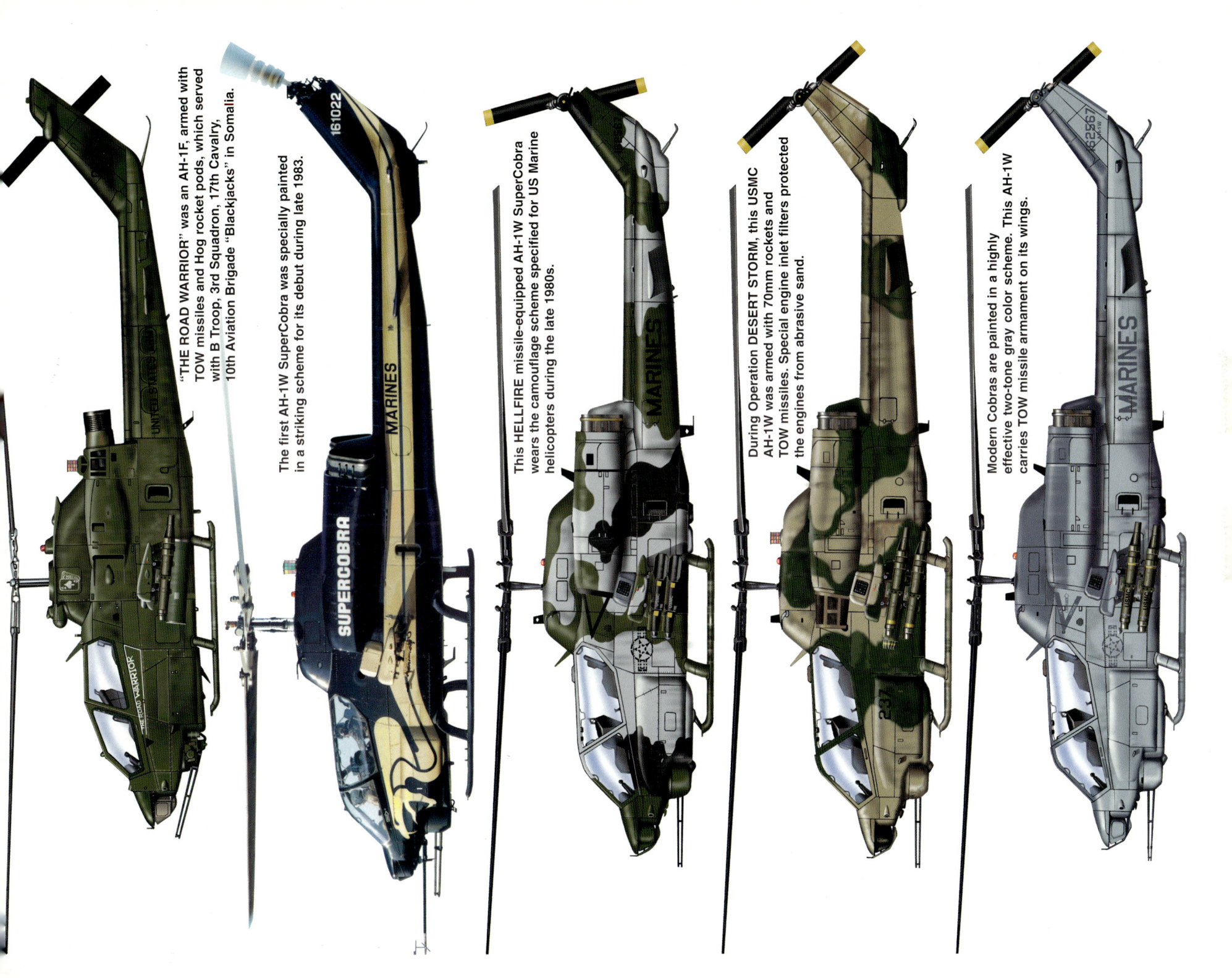

"THE ROAD WARRIOR" was an AH-1F, armed with TOW missiles and Hog rocket pods, which served with B Troop, 3rd Squadron, 17th Cavalry, 10th Aviation Brigade "Blackjacks" in Somalia.

The first AH-1W SuperCobra was specially painted in a striking scheme for its debut during late 1983.

This HELLFIRE missile-equipped AH-1W SuperCobra wears the camouflage scheme specified for US Marine helicopters during the late 1980s.

During Operation DESERT STORM, this USMC AH-1W was armed with 70mm rockets and TOW missiles. Special engine inlet filters protected the engines from abrasive sand.

Modern Cobras are painted in a highly effective two-tone gray color scheme. This AH-1W carries TOW missile armament on its wings.

(Left) The addition of target acquisition components to the belly of the AH-1S required that the landing lights be relocated onto the skid cross tube. (Author)

The 90 degree tail rotor gearbox is housed in a large teardrop fairing on the AH-1S. (Author)

(Below left) Guides were added to the AH-1S canopy frame as part of the wire strike protection kit. (Author)

(Below right) The AH-1S exhaust system. (Author)

Mounted atop the AH-1S canopy was a wire-cutting blade, part of a kit deemed necessary in view of the helicopter's low level environment. The gunner's armored seat panels were significantly smaller than those of the pilot. (Author)

The AH-1S gunner's TOW sighting unit. "Armchair" flight controls are visible along with a cockpit light attached to the armored seat side panel. (Keith Lovern)

This sand colored AH-1F began life as an AH-1G. The teardrop fairing just forward of the engine intake houses fire control system components. (via Terry Love)

The four tube TOW installation on an AH-1S, (77-22805). (Lennart Lundh)

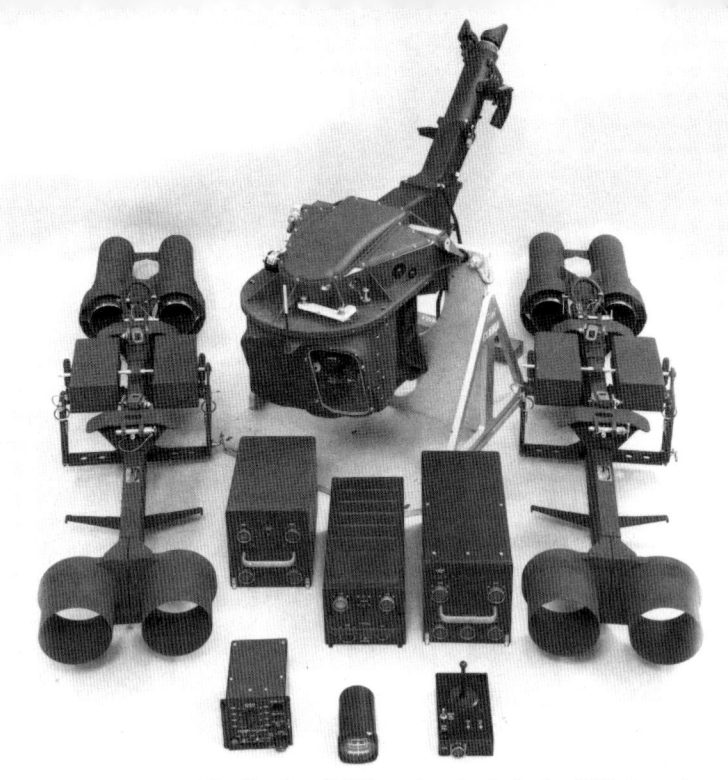

The major components of the Hughes TOW system include the TSU, launchers, electronic units (center) and aircrew controls. (Bell)

An AH-1F armed with TOW missiles. The omni directional airspeed system extending from the cockpit frame provides input for cannon and rocket accuracy. (Bell)

An AH-1F (79-23241) of the 268th Attack Helicopter Battery at Ft Lewis, Washington during 1986. (Don Abrahamson via Terry Love)

The 1,800 shp T53-L-703 engine was the standard installation for the AH-1S series. (Bell)

An AH-1F fires 70mm rockets during evaluation of the armament. (Bell)

AH-1F of the California National Guard, armed with a 19-shot rocket pod and single-cell TOW launchers (four missiles). A dust and sand screen has been added to the engine inlet. The Airborne Laser Tracker, mounted on the leading edge of the rotor pylon, not only searches for, locks onto, and tracks a target, but displays the data on the cockpit heads-up display (HUD) and cues the TSU to the target. (Skip Robinson)

AH-1S Cobras, minus their wings, of the 147th Aviation Battalion, Wisconsin National Guard, await their fate, having been replaced by Sikorsky UH-60 "Blackhawks." Until the mid 1990s, AH-1S variants served with the National Guard of 21 states. (Author)

Main Rotor Blade Development

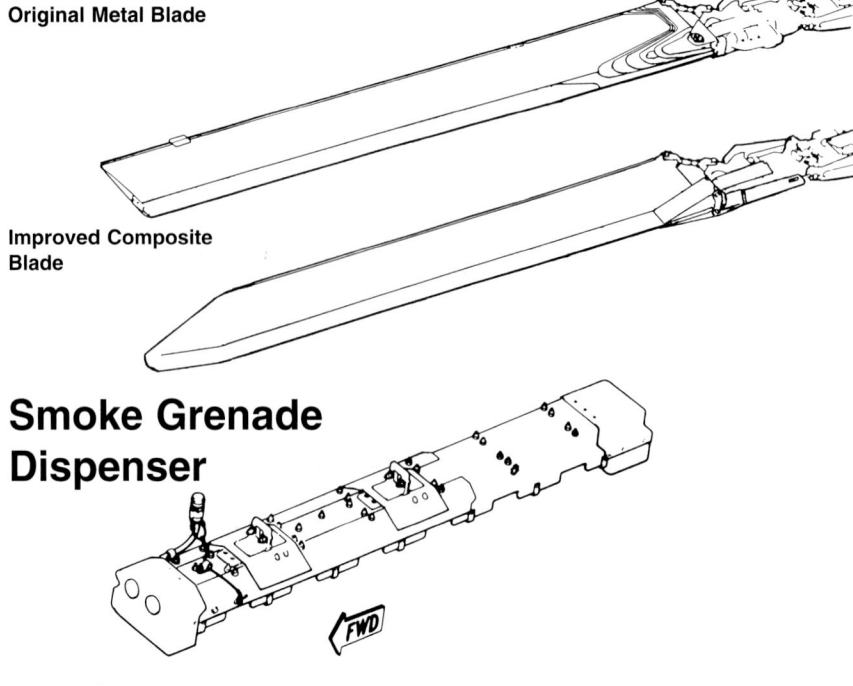

Original Metal Blade

Improved Composite Blade

Smoke Grenade Dispenser

The first production AH-IG (66-15249) served as a TH-IG with the 9th Infantry Division at Ft Lewis, Washington during 1972. The light-colored panels are Orange-Yellow and a divisional emblem appears where the turret barrel openings have been faired over. (AAHS)

Army Cobra Trainer Variants

A number of early AH-lGs, including the first production Cobra, were converted to full control dual TH-1Gs by having their gunner's abbreviated flight controls replaced with complete controls and instruments. As part of the "Minuteman" program during the mid 1980s, Bell modified 15 TH-lGs to TH-1S(MOD) aircraft for the Army National Guard.

After all AH-1Gs had been converted to AH-1S(MC)s by mid 1982, the Army later modified 41 as TAH-1F trainers by adding a cyclic hydraulic booster and a master armament safety switch to the instructor's front cockpit. Prior to that time, all AH-lS variants used as crew trainers at Ft Rucker were known as TH-lSs. The designation TAH-1S identified ten Cobras modified with the AH-64 Pilot Night Vision System (PNVS) for use as surrogate trainers for AH-64 pilots at Ft Rucker.

By 1990, ten original AH-lGs still in the Army inventory were removed from flying status following their conversion to electrical and armament trainers.

AH-1T

Essentially a descendant of the Model 309 KingCobra, the AH-lT incorporated features of the AH-1J airframe, Model 214 dynamics, upgraded engines and KingCobra technology. The AH-1T represented a necessary evolutionary development of the AH-1J with the advent of the Hughes TOW (Tube-launched, Optically-tracked, Wire-guided) missile. The conversion to TOW capability meant a number of changes to the AH-1J airframe, foremost of which was a 12 inch fuselage extension (immediately aft of the cockpit) to counterbalance the additional weight of electronic countermeasure equipment, necessary for the anti-armor mission. Outwardly, the "Tango" was distinguished from the AH-1J mainly by the broken symmetry of the lower tail boom plane and the addition of a ventral fin for stability.

Model 214 dynamics included a 48 foot diameter main rotor with 33 inch chord blades, and a larger 8 foot 8 inch tail rotor which was mounted atop the tail fin, similar to the UH-1 "Huey" arrangement.

Since the TOW installation reduced the SeaCobra's performance and the AH-1T weighed two tons more than its predecessor, the switch was made to a Pratt & Whitney T400-WV-402 Twin Pack rated at 1,970shp for takeoff. With its gross weight increased to 14,000 pounds, the AH-1T could lift 5,400 pounds of fuel and ordnance, more than twice that of its AH-1J predecessor.

Bell was notified to proceed with modifications of the last two production AH-lJs in the Spring of 1974, which were eventually brought up to full AH-1T standards. The first prototype made its maiden flight on 20 May 1976. The Marine Corps ordered 55 machines, the first 33 of which were delivered without TOW, but later fitted. The first example (159228) was accepted by the Marine Corps on 15 October 1977 and deliveries to HMA-269 began during early December of 1978.

To boost the Tango's performance, Bell began development of an advanced variant during 1978. A bailed USMC AH-1T was mated with a GE T700-401 Twin Pack rated at 3,250shp. The 15,000 pound prototype first flew in April 1980 attaining a speed of 193 mph. After two months of evaluation by Navy and Marine test pilots, the "SuperCobra" was returned to its original configuration when a lack of funds prohibited advancement of the project.

By the end of 1984, the AH-1T order was nearly complete with 23 aircraft TOW equipped. Bell was contracted to retrofit the remainder, the first of which was delivered during early 1983. Within that time frame, the procurement of 44 improved SuperCobras for the Marine Corps was approved.

Later that year, another AH-1T (161022) was used to reach a milestone in the Cobra's lineage. Known as the AH-1T Plus SuperCobra, and painted in a striking snake motif, the devel-

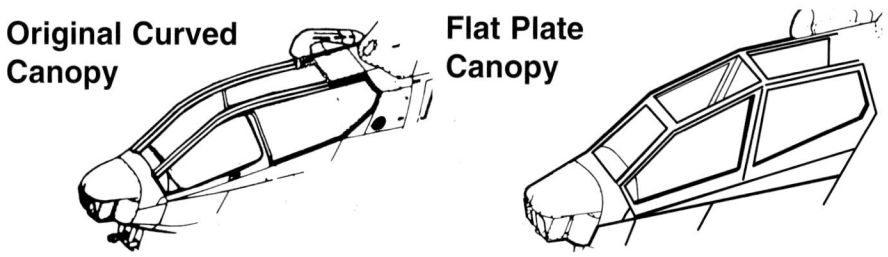

Original Curved Canopy   **Flat Plate Canopy**

(Left) A TAH-1F during late 1983. Ballast replaced the turret weapons and International Orange was applied on the nose, fuselage and elevators. (Ted Paskowski via Terry Love)

AH-1Ts without the TOW system were called "Slicks." The 33 acquired by the Marine Corps were later fitted with M65 TOW systems. This, the first AH-1T (which was actually the second to the last AH-1J produced) evaluates a "heavy" armament load of 76 rockets. (Bell)

opment and test variant made its first flight on 16 November. Powered by the T700-401 engines developed for the Navy's Sikorsky SH-60, the AH-1T Plus boasted a 65 percent increase in power over the standard AH-1T.

After successful tests with AIM-9L air-to-air missiles at China Lake during 1982, the Marines insisted that their AH-1T Plus be Sidewinder-equipped. Budget constraints again came into play and although AIM-9Ls were in Marine Corps inventory, their production had ceased, resulting in only brief appearances mounted outboard on the improved Tango's stub wings. Approval for procurement of the improved AH-1T, which evolved into the AH-1W, was given in May 1984.

An AH-1T "Slick" was capable of accepting a wide range of armament, much of which is seen on display at the Naval Air Test Center. (Bell)

A badly weathered AH-1T of HML/A-167 undergoes maintenance. The AH-1T's "TwinPac" powerplant is the same engine configuration used to power the "International AH-1J." (USMC)

A Tactical Aircrew Combat Training System (TACTS) pod is affixed to the air-to-air missile launch rail of an AH-1T at Camp Pendelton. The pod provides aircraft and weapons data to ground tracking stations during air-to-air training flights. (USMC)

To give the AH-1W night targeting capability, Bell integrated a Texas Instruments FLIR into the nose of an AH-1T (159228) during the early 1980s. Called the "Viper", the sight system never went beyond the research stage. (Bell)

A pair of AH-1Ts carry out a test flight prior to delivery. Both are TOW-equipped and finished in Dark Desert Tan. (Bell)

An AH-1T of HMA-169 in Field Green with black markings. (Douglas E. Slowiak via Terry Love)

AH-1W Whiskey Cobra

Since the 530 pound TOW installation hampered performance of the AH-1T, plans had been made as early as 1974 to upgrade the -402 engine. In view of Marine budget constraints, Bell offered to demonstrate the feasibility of integrating a pair of General Electric T700-401 engines with a 2,350shp combining gearbox into an AH-1T airframe. The Marines loaned an AH-1T to Bell during November 1979 for modification and turned it over to the Navy for evaluation the following October. Although tests yielded superior performance ratings, the project was shelved due to lack of funds. After aircraft attrition combined with the AH-1T's weak performance in hot and high regions to severely strain Marine Rapid Deployment Force obligations, and after repeated funding rejections, the government finally gave the Navy the go ahead to mate the new engines with an AH-1T order scheduled for 1984-85. The result was the AH-1T Plus which led to a contract for 22 aircraft to be delivered during 1985.

Following successful evaluations, during which a top speed of 199 mph was achieved, a second batch of 22 was ordered. So drastic was the deviation from the original AH-1T design that the SuperCobra was redesignated AH-1W (known simply as "Whiskey") during production. Not only were changes made in power plant but also in armament. With the introduction of the HELLFIRE missile, the AH-1W became the only attack helicopter with dual anti-armor capability.

Since the Marines decided to capitalize on existent AH-1T technology, they were able to forego the costly and time-consuming process of developing and breaking in a new design. Deliveries began during March 1986 with completion of the order scheduled for 1988. The first AH-1W was placed in service with HMLA-169. Plans were also made to bring 37 AH-1Ts up to Whiskey standards by 1990. The Marine Corps set its sights on a force of 230 AH-1Ws by the end of 1997, including both production and converted aircraft.

Billed as the most powerful and versatile attack helicopter in the world, the Whiskey Cobra offers the widest array of weapons and the highest power-to-weight ratio. Backing up Bell Helicopter's belief that, "There is no such thing as second place", the AH-1W can hover out of ground effect at 3,000 feet with a full armament load and, with an air-to-air ordnance load, climb at more than 800 feet per minute on one engine; its normal rate of climb is 2,000 feet per minute (with both engines). Efficient as it is effective, the Whiskey also boasts the lowest maintenance requirements of any attack helicopter. Protective measures include crew armor, dual radar warning, infrared jammers, dual chaff/flare dispensers and a fuel system designed to survive 23mm shell hits.

Empty weight of the AH-1W is 10,300 pounds with a maximum gross weight of 14,750 pounds. The twin GE T700-401 power plant, rated at 3,380shp, drives a 48-foot diameter, semi-rigid, bonded metal main rotor. At sea level, the Whiskey cruises at 170 mph and has a maximum speed of nearly 200 mph. As the largest Cobra variant, the AH-1W measures 45 feet, 6 inches from nose to tail with a height of 14 feet, 3 inches.

The Marine SuperCobra is unequaled in the variety of firepower it can deliver. It is the only attack helicopter to feature dual anti-armor capability with HELLFIRE and TOW missiles. The AH-1W uses the AGM-114 HELLFIRE to knock out heavy armor and hardened targets at ranges exceeding four miles. Introduced during 1995, HELLFIRE is a laser-guided missile weighing 105 pounds, 20 pounds of which is a blast fragmentation warhead. Four AGM-114s are carried on a launcher mounted to the outboard station of the left wing. When fired in the cooperative mode, with laser target illumination from a source other than the helicopter itself, the crew can fire the missile and quickly evade, which is known as "fire and forget". The crew

The prototype AH-1W "SuperCobra" was given a striking paint scheme to emphasize its venomous characteristics. (Bell)

can also lock on to a target with an onboard laser designator. This can be accomplished with a Night Targeting System (NTS), which uses forward-looking infrared (FLIR) to detect and attack targets at night, in adverse weather conditions or in smoke. The first NTS-equipped AH-1Ws deployed with the 26th Marine Expeditionary Unit to Bosnia during late 1996.

If faced with environmental conditions that would hamper the laser-guided HELLFIRE, the combat-proven, wire-guided TOW can be utilized at ranges of nearly two miles. An improved version, called TOW II, can penetrate reactive armor adapted to tanks. Once the TOW missile is fired, flight command signals are fed through a fine wire that unravels from the missile. Although that makes it nearly impervious to jamming, the missile must be tracked until impact, exposing the aircraft during the missile's flight.

The Whiskey's air-to-air fighting capability is derived from the AIM-9L Sidewinder and Stinger missiles. Though both are heat-seekers, the decision on which to use is based upon the battlefield terrain and type of adversary aircraft. To meet an attack by a fast fixed-wing aircraft, the Sidewinder would be the likely choice since it has greater range, is faster, has a larger warhead and a proximity fuse. The Stinger, on the other hand, with its contact fuse, is best for taking out enemy helicopters.

The multi-mission AH-1W can also carry the AGM-65 Maverick and AGM-22A Sidearm (anti-radiation) missiles. A wide assortment of standard 70mm (2.75-inch) rockets, including those with submunitions warheads, can also be carried. Basic rocket load outs comprise the LAU-68 launcher which holds 7 rockets and the LAU-61 which holds 19. Additional options include 5 inch Zuni rockets, GPU-2A 20mm gun pods, MK-81 and Mk-82 bombs, CBU-55B fuel-air explosives, M-118 smoke grenade dispenser, SUU-44 flare dispenser and 78 or 100-gallon auxiliary fuel tanks. A carryover from the AH-1J and AH-1T is the M197 20mm rotary cannon in the nose turret, which is controlled by crew helmet sights or the TSU. At the onset of AH-1W production, the M197 was qualified to fire the Phalanx round, a powerful projectile

An early AH-1W fires 5 inch rockets during tests. Cameras were mounted on the forward skids to record the evaluations. (Bell)

The AH-1W's offset trailing edge of the vertical fin combined with the cambered tail to offset torque induced yaw. (Bell)

Among the SuperCobra's impressive arsenal are Sidewinder and Sidearm missiles. (Bell)

that combines depleted uranium with tungsten steel, with twice the velocity of the M-57 round to penetrate armor.

Marine aviation currently operates four Marine Aircraft Wings, three of which are assigned AH-1Ws. Subordinate to the MAWs are Marine Aircraft Groups (MAGs) which comprise light helicopter squadrons, known as HMLAs (Helicopter, Marine, Light Attack). These units operate both AH-1Ws and heavily armed UH-1N twin Hueys for close-in fire support. The 2nd MAW manages two HMLAs, the 4th MAW (Reserve) has three and the 3rd MAW boasts five, one of which is a training squadron. The latter, a Fleet Replacement Squadron designated HMT-303, trains Navy and Marine AH-1W and HH/UH-1N crew members.

2nd MAW
MAG-26
HMLA-167	"Warriors"	TV

MAG-29
HMLA-269	"Sea Cobras"	HF

3rd MAW
MAG-39
HMLA-169	"Vipers"	SN
HMLA-267	"Black Aces"	UV
HMLA-367	"Scarface"	VT
HMLA-369	"Gunfighters"	SM
HMT-303	"Atlas"	QT

4th MAW
MAG-42
HMLA-773	"Cobras"	MP
HMLA-767		MM
HMLA-775	"Coyotes"	WR

AH-1W Hellfire Missile Launcher

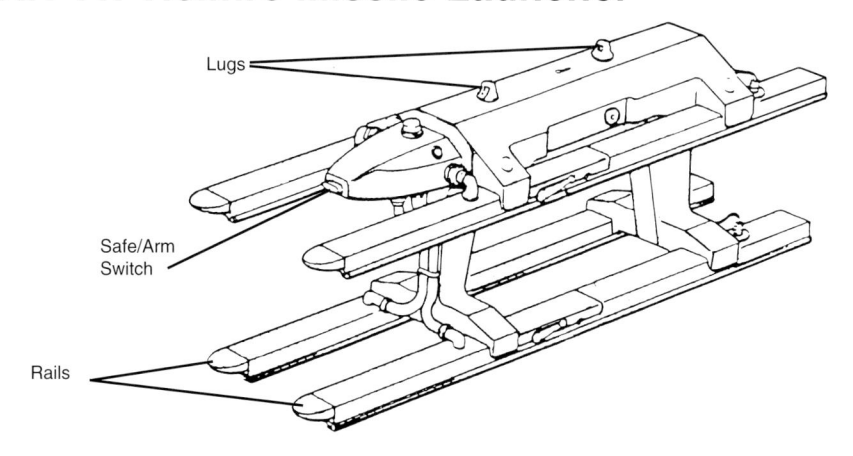

The AH-1W retained the original Cobra's curved canopy. The prototype is seen carrying Sidearm missiles mounted to the outboard stations. (Bell)

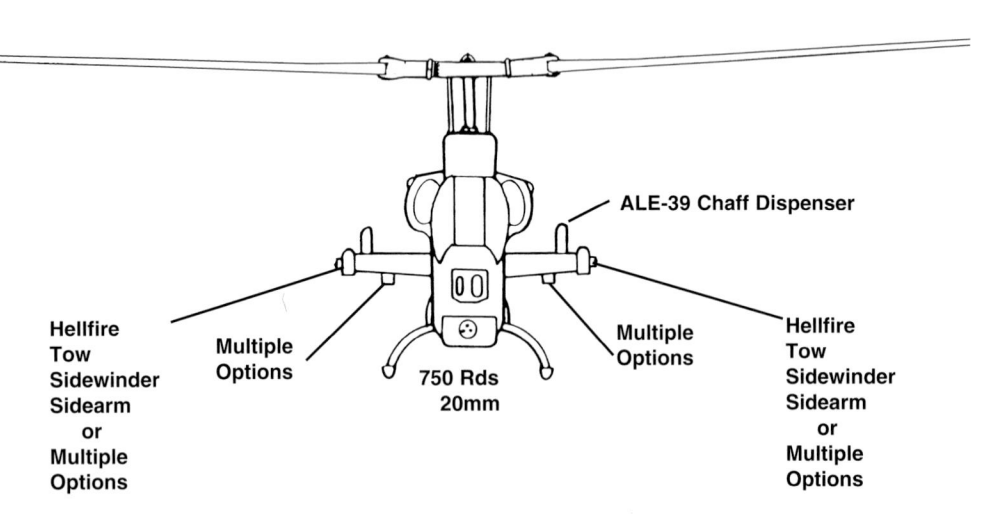

One of four E-Systems AN/APR-39 radar warning antennas (above the rescue arrow) that was installed on later Cobras. (Bell)

The Hellfire missile system was initially developed for the U.S. Army's AH-64 Apache helicopter. Here it is paired up with a 7 shot rocket pod on an AH-1W. HMM-266 became a CH-46 squadron and the "Warriors" became HMLA-167 equipped with AH-1Ws. (US. Army)

AH-1 Multi-Mission Armament and Stores

- Hellfire Tow Sidewinder Sidearm or Multiple Options
- Multiple Options
- 750 Rds 20mm
- Multiple Options
- ALE-39 Chaff Dispenser
- Hellfire Tow Sidewinder Sidearm or Multiple Options

36

Head-on view of the Hellfire missile system and position of the AN/ALE-39 chaff/flare dispenser. (Bell)

This gray and green camouflaged AH-1W of HMLA-269 carries a pair of long range fuel tanks on the outboard pylons. (David F Brown via Terry Love)

A Light Sand camouflaged AH-1W of HMLA-169 with open engine and transmission access panels. (MAP)

A Sidearm missile equipped AH-1W. The chaff/flare dispenser cartridge has been removed from the launcher on the wing. (Bell)

37

The AH-1W prototype firing an AGM-114 Hellfire missile. (Bell)

An AH-1W unleashes a Maverick air-to-ground missile during evaluations of the system. (Bell)

An AH-1W of HMLA-167 "Warriors" fires an AGM-122 Sidearm missile. The Sidearm was designed for use against air defense radars and is a derivative of the AIM-9C Sidewinder air-to-air missile. (Bell)

A Hellfire and rocket-armed SuperCobra goes through a hover check prior to takeoff. (Bell)

A two-tone gray AH-1W with subdued markings. The rectangular shape on the fuselage underside houses a navigation antenna. (Bell)

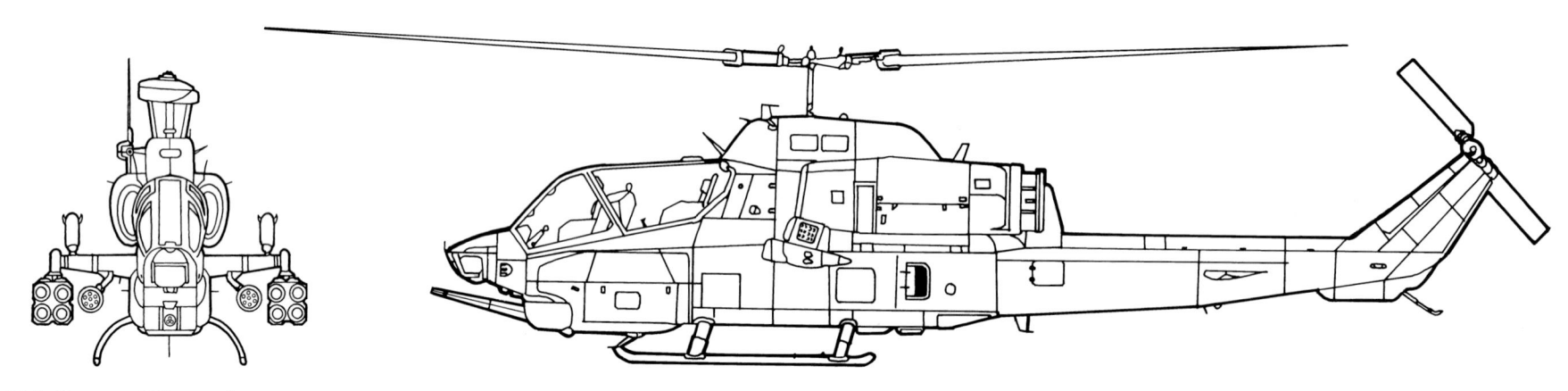

AH-1W Specifications

Length (Fuselage)	45 ft.
Height	14 ft. 2 in.
Main Rotor Diameter	48 ft.
Tail Rotor Diameter	8 ft. 8 in.
Empty Weight	10,300lbs
Maximum Gross Weight	14,750lbs
Powerplant	Two T700-401 General Electric 3,380 shp engines
Armament	TOW missiles, HELLFIRE missiles 70mm rockets, 5 inch rockets, 20mm cannon, Sidewinder and Stinger missiles, Maverick and Sidearm missiles, Multipurpose stores.
Cruise Speed	170 mph
Service Ceiling	18,000 ft.
Range	280 nautical miles
Crew	2

One of the first flights with Bell's Advanced 680 four bladed rotor system during early 1989. A 19 shot rocket pod occupies the outboard wing station. The "VX5" on the forward tail boom denotes assignment to Air Test and Evaluation Squadron Five. (Bell)

AH-1-4BW

So successful is the AH-lW in Marine aviation that a three phase plan was drawn up to re-manufacture the SuperCobra to vastly improve its performance and operational effectiveness, and thereby extending its life for another quarter of a century. At the heart of this three-phase program is a four-bladed rotor system. While the four-bladed Whiskey has the same bloodlines as its Cobra predecessors, it represents a quantum leap in technology. A new drive train, tail boom and four-bladed pusher tail rotor is expected to increase payload by more than 1,000 pounds, add 20 knots more speed, increase climb rate and allow a higher hover altitude. Greater responsiveness and agility mean an 80 percent increase in the new variant's functional flight envelope.

Bell began work on rotor hubs and blade constructed of composite materials during the late 1970s. By 1982, a composite, bearingless and hingeless rotor system had been developed, which was tested in a four-bladed configuration on a Bell Model 222 in 1985. After the first AH-1T loaned to Bell by the Marine Corps was converted to an AH-lW (161022), it was fitted with the four-blade Model 680 rotor. Designated AH-l-4BW (a Four-Bladed Whiskey), it began test flights on 24 January 1989.

The semi-folding rotor system is 15 percent lighter than contemporary systems has 50 percent fewer parts, reduces vibration by 70 percent and is a remarkable improvement in ballistic survivability. Equally impressive are the aerobatic attributes of the -4BW which include such high G maneuvers as rolls, loops, split-S turns, hammerhead stalls and maximum rate roll reversals.

A completely revised cockpit will feature a fourth generation digital automatic flight control system (DAFCS), which enhances handling qualities with added system safety. Other cockpit enhancements include multi-function displays, mission data loader, systems monitors and diagnostics. The -4BW will also receive upgraded landing gear, pylon structural modifications and an APU housed in the rotor pylon. Two wing stations will be added for a total of six, allowing the Cobra to carry 16 precision guided munitions, which translates to complete air-to-ground and air-to-air capability.

Other improvements include an onboard Global Positioning System (GPS), additional detection and countermeasures gear, such as laser warning, missile warning and engine IR suppressors, and an Airborne Target Handover System that can work in conjunction with other aircraft.

The -4BW has an empty weight of 12,200 pounds and weighs in at 18,500 pounds at maximum gross weight. Its range is nearly 400 miles.

The AH-l-4BW exhibits its impressive performance capabilities. (Bell)

The Marine Corps plans to upgrade 180 AH-1Ws to meet their expanding mission requirement and keep the Cobra in service as their prime attack helicopter until 2025, when a joint service replacement is due to emerge. Under the title "H-1 Upgrade", the SuperCobra's new lease on life was planned as a two-part program in conjunction with a similar upgrade of the USMC UH-1N Twin Huey, of which 100 will be remanufacture. Both types will share identical rotor systems, drive trains, engines, transmissions, hydraulics, electrical systems and tail booms. Not only does that commonality mean extreme cost-effectiveness, but unprecedented maintenance and logistic support benefits. The engineering phase was underway during 1997 with the first AH-1-4BW due for evaluation during 1998. Delivery is slated to begin during late 1999.

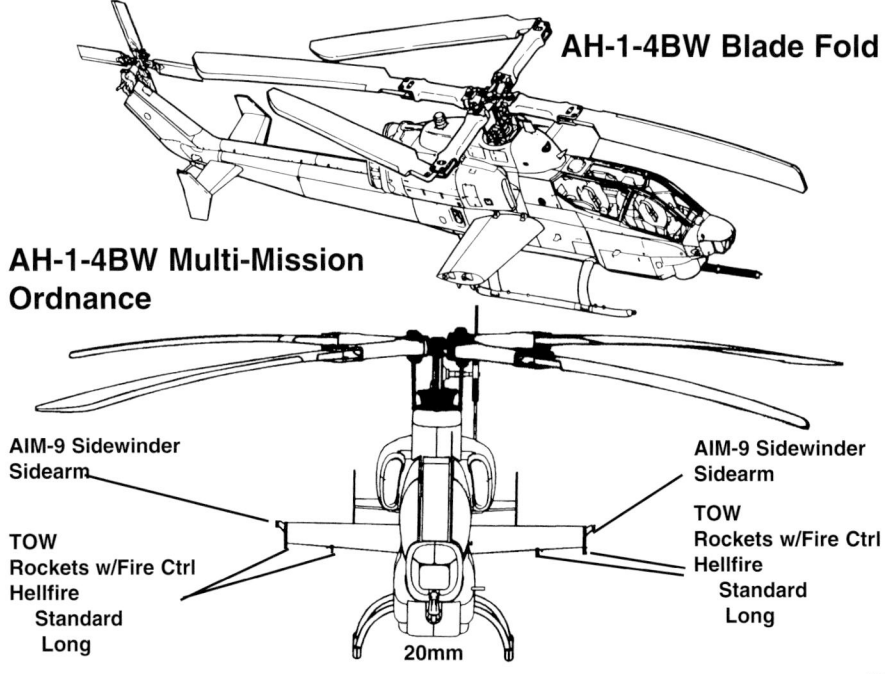

AH-1-4BW Blade Fold

AH-1-4BW Multi-Mission Ordnance

AIM-9 Sidewinder
Sidearm

TOW
Rockets w/Fire Ctrl
Hellfire
Standard
Long

20mm
750 rounds W/Fire ctrl

AIM-9 Sidewinder
Sidearm

TOW
Rockets w/Fire Ctrl
Hellfire
Standard
Long

A U.S. Army AH-1F lifts off Point Salines Airfield, Grenada during OPERATION URGENT FURY. (USAF)

Worldwide Conflict

Cobras are a natural presence at world trouble spots where U.S. forces defend American interests. When U.S. Marines served as members of the multinational peace keeping force in Lebanon during the 1980s, they brought AH-1J SeaCobras to patrol the volatile region.

OPERATION URGENT FURY identified the October 1983 invasion of the island of Grenada in the Caribbean basin. The main assault on Grenada was carried out by U.S. Army and Marine helicopter units. Marine Squadron HMM-261 and HML-167 embarked aboard the USS GUAM with AH-1T SeaCobras for CH-46 escort, infantry support and anti-armor missions. Armed with TOW missiles, 20mm cannon and 2.75-inch rockets, the SeaCobras proved their worth in air support, however, two AH-1Ts were downed by intense anti-aircraft fire with a loss of three crew members.

AH-1S Cobras were among the mix of Army helicopters deployed: D Company, 82nd Combat Aviation Battalion, 82nd Airborne Division and B Troop, 1st Squadron, 17th Cavalry, both based at Ft Bragg, North Carolina. Armed like their Marine counterparts, the AH-1Ss mainly flew escort for UH-60 troop-carrying and Medevac helicopters. As the largest U.S. combat action since the end of the Vietnam war, URGENT FURY illustrated the value of heavily-armed helicopters.

During the Gulf war, an increase in attacks on shipping and oil terminals during 1987 prompted a U.S. response, titled OPERATION EARNEST WILL, that included four AH-1Ts. The Cobras were among various types of helicopters that equipped HMM-263, which embarked aboard the USS GUADALCANAL. During October, the Cobras sank three patrol boats which had fired at an Army special operations helicopter. That month, six AH-1Ws of HMLA-69 at Camp Pendleton embarked aboard the USS OKINAWA for round-the-clock protection of shipping lanes in the Persian Gulf. One of the AH-1Ts was shot down by Iran's Islamic Revolutionary Guard Corps during April 1988.

U.S. Army Cobras were also present in Honduras during 1988 as part of the U.S. exercise task force DRAGON/GOLDEN PHEASANT, intended to help discourage Nicaraguan forces from entering Honduras.

In accordance with USMC rapid deployment policy, Cobras were among the more than 200 aircraft sent to support ground units during the first deployment of OPERATION DESERT SHIELD. The helicopters of Marine Air Group 16 (MAG-16) were stripped down and flown by USAF C-5s to Saudi Arabia's Abdul Aziz Naval Base. MAG-16's Cobra assets comprised AH-1Ws of HMLA-369 based at MCAS Camp Pendleton, California and HMLA-367 at MCAS Futema, Okinawa. Additional Cobras arrived in the Persian Gulf during September aboard U.S. Navy Amphibious Group 2, marking the first time a general purpose assault ship launched U.S. aircraft in combat. Aboard the USS NASSAU (LHA-4) were AH-1Ws of HMLA-269, which set up shop at Dhahran Royal Saudi Air Force Air Base.

Reserve attack squadron HMA-775 of MAG-26, based at Camp Pendleton, brought AH-1Js into the conflict, operating from Abdul Aziz. Completing the Marine Corps force was MAG-50 of the 5th MEB, which embarked with five helicopter squadrons aboard the USS TARAWA (LHA-1) and USS NEW ORLEANS (LPH-11). Two of the squadrons operated Cobras: HMLA-169 from MCAS Camp Pendleton with AH-1Ws, and Reserve HMA-773 from NAS Atlanta with AH-1Js. HMLA-367 and HMLA-369 operated from land bases, while HMLA-169 and HMLA-269 flew from naval ships. A total of 91 USMC Cobras were committed to the conflict: 60 AH-1Ws and 24 AH-1Js, plus 7 AH-1Ts on loan from HMLA-267. The AH-1Js and AH-1Ts were put to use as transport escorts after relinquishing anti-armor duty to the more capable AH-1Ws.

Besides their 20mm cannon, muscle for the Marine Cobras consisted primarily of LAU-68 seven tube pods on the inboard station for firing 2.75 inch Hydra air-to-ground rockets. The same mounts were used to carry CBU-55 fuel-air explosives (FAE). Carried on the outboard stations were either BGM-71 TOW missiles, AGM-114 Hellfire anti-tank missiles or AGM-122A Sidearm anti-radiation missiles.

Cobras, along with other Marine helicopters, operated from forward sites in support of the 1st and 2nd Marine Divisions. A nearly equal number of helicopters, with the 4th and 5th MEBs, flew from ships in the Persian Gulf. Fuel and munitions were pre-positioned at forward operating sites, which gave the Cobras extreme latitude to attack targets. Others maintained pressure on Iraqi forces throughout the region by rendezvousing with fuel and munitions carrying CH-53s deep in the war zone. Marine Cobras also took advantage of their own or Army fuel trucks in forward areas. Throughout DESERT STORM, Marine "Whiskey" Cobras proved to be a devastating force in the U.S. arsenal, with a final tally of 97 tanks, 104 APCs and vehicles, 16 bunkers and 2 AA sites destroyed.

True to their expertise in airmobile concepts, the U.S. Army also dispatched swarms of helicopters to the Middle East during DESERT SHIELD. Army leaders had learned to integrate helicopters with ground units during the Vietnam war. Having honed their skills for a quarter of a century, the Army was ready for a massive helicopter deployment in the Middle East.

Taking their place among the wide range of Army helicopters were over 140 AH-1S vari-

The first C-5 to arrive at Kissmayu, Somalia dwarfs an AH-1F of B Troop, 3rd Squadron, 17th Cavalry, 10th Aviation brigade. (Anthony Salerno)

ants. Since superior Iraqi armor was an immediate concern, the deployment of anti-armor helicopter forces were given top priority. First to go was the 82nd Aviation Brigade of the 82nd Airborne Division, which fielded one dozen AH-1Fs at Dhahran. In mid September of DESERT SHIELD, the unique 101st Airborne Division (Air Assault), with its enormous helicopter inventory, arrived aboard Navy transport ships. As the largest aviation brigade, which boasts ten battalions, the 101st has a Cobra attack battalion and a cavalry squadron with AH-1s and OH-58s. Beginning in January 1991, Cobras began arriving with the 1st and 24th Infantry Divisions and the 503rd Battalion of the 3rd Armored Division.

Shortly after their arrival in Saudi Arabia, U.S. Army helicopter units dispersed to remote airstrips to acclimate themselves with the severe desert conditions. Once operational, they moved troops and supplies and attacked enemy armor. Like their Marine counterparts, Army Cobras used forward refueling and rearming sites to greatly expand their operating areas.

Foremost among the hazards encountered by Marine and Army Cobras in the Middle East were horrendous sand and heat conditions as well as ground fire. Since helicopter training flights in Saudi Arabia were limited to a 500-foot altitude to avoid proximity to fixed-wing aircraft, helicopter exposure to sand was greatly increased. Despite the abrasive qualities of sand, Cobras maintained a high degree of serviceability. Of greater concern was Iraqi anti-aircraft systems, which included 23mm and 57mm cannon, plus shoulder-fired air-defense weapons. Also looming in aircrews' minds was the existence of more than 5,000 enemy armored vehicles, each with a heavy anti-aircraft machine gun. Cobras successfully countered these threats with sophisticated onboard systems and by staying out of range and flying at extremely low altitudes.

Three Cobras were lost during the entire campaign, two of which were non-combat losses, while the third occurred during the postwar period. An Army AH-1 went down with mechanical problems on 22 January 1991 and the crew was recovered. On 2 February 1991, an AH-1J of HMA-775 crashed during an escort mission in Saudi Arabia, killing both crewmen. The same unit suffered another AH-1J loss on 6 March, which left the crew injured. Bell engineers wasted no time in applying experience gained during the conflict to the Cobra's ongoing development process.

In view of their ability to "carry a big stick", Cobras invariably ended up at other world trouble spots. During late May of 1990, the 22nd Marine Expeditionary Unit set sail aboard the amphibious assault ship USS SAIPAN for Monrovia, Liberia in response to threats to U.S. citizens during fighting between government and rebel forces. The mission, dubbed OPERATION SHARP EDGE, was a superior display of Navy-Marine special operations intended to protect and evacuate U.S. citizens. Included among the units rushed to the area was HMM-261, equipped with AH-1Ts.

On 5 August, the task force closed to within six miles of the Liberian capital and launched CH-46 and CH-53 transports toward the landing zones. HMM-261's Cobras orbited all three landing zones to provide fire support. Though intense fighting between the warring factions took place throughout the two-week rescue mission, the evacuation of more than 1,600 U.S. citizens and foreign nationals was completed under tense conditions without incident. It would not be the Cobra's last trip to Africa.

During January 1991, it became necessary for a Marine helicopter force to evacuate the American embassy in the capital city of Mogadishu, Somalia. The continuing brutal conflict in the region exacted an enormous toll, prompting UN intervention beginning in early 1993. American and UN troops sent to the area, on what was to be a humanitarian mission, found themselves pitted against Somali warlords who led heavily-armed clans.

Shortly after its arrival the U.S. Army's 10th Aviation Brigade from Ft Drum, New York

"THE ROAD WARRIOR", an AH-1F of the 10th Aviation Brigade, takes on fuel at a forward refueling site during OPERATION RESTORE HOPE. (Anthony Salerno)

spearheaded the Army aviation portion of OPERATION RESTORE HOPE during January 1993. The brigade's 3rd Squadron, 17th Cavalry (3/17), B Troop, equipped with AH-1Fs and OH-58 scout helicopters, was positioned at Kissmayu in Somalia's southern sector to control two warlords. Nicknamed "Task Force Bandit", the unit went on the attack to effectively put the more persistent warlord out of business. By March the U.S. Army and Marines had nearly 100 helicopters in Somalia, the majority of them based at Baledogle's Soviet-built airfield. A total of 65 Army choppers, including AH-1Fs, formed "Task Force Falcon", which was headquartered at Baledogle. The Marines deployed AH-1W equipped HMM-164, which operated from the USS TRIPOLI (LPH-10) off Mogadishu's shore.

Early in the campaign, Cobras provided protection and support for infantry air assaults into four towns. A great deal of their time was then spent with reconnaissance and covering troop resupply missions and food relief sites. Although hostilities continued, a large loss of American lives during a raid in October brought the U. S. helicopter commitment to a halt by the Spring of 1994.

Beginning in September 1994, Marine and Army Cobras flew missions in support of U. S. troops deployed to Haiti as part of the U. S. effort to re-power the Haitian president. Almost half of the 107 U. S. Army helicopters deployed during OPERATION UPHOLD DEMOCRACY belonged to the 10th Aviation Brigade, which embarked aboard the carrier USS Dwight D Eisenhower (CVN-69). The Brigade's 2/25th Attack Helicopter Battalion brought its com-

An AH-1F of the 10th Aviation Brigade is lashed to the deck of the USS DWIGHT D EISENHOWER for OPERATION UPHOLD DEMOCRACY in Haiti during 1994. Besides the turret cannon, this Cobra is armed with TOW missiles and "Hog" rocket pods. The "bandit" on the rotor pylon may have been a carryover from the unit's previous assignment to Task Force Bandit in Somalia. The carrier's name was applied to the tail boom. (U.S. Army)

10th Aviation Brigade AH-1Fs deployed to Haiti aboard the USS DWIGHT D EISENHOWER. (US Army)

plement of 14 AH-1Fs for the five month operation.

U. S. Military involvement in Bosnia and Herzegovina received little attention until the downing of USAF Captain Scott O'Grady's F-16 on 2 June 1995. The shoot-down and rescue of O'Grady reigned in the media and captivated the American public. U. S. Marine AH-1W Cobras were prime players in the rescue of "Basher 52" from hostile northwestern Bosnia.

Due to rising tension and increased conflict in the region, the amphibious assault ship KEARSARGE (LHD-3) had been positioned in the Adriatic Sea to provide a presence and prepare for rescue missions in conjunction with UN OPERATION DENY FLIGHT. Aboard the KEARSARGE was the 24th Marine Expeditionary Unit, whose organic air assets comprised AV-8B Harriers, CH-53 Super Stallions and three AH-1W Cobras of HMLA-269. When it was discovered that O'Grady was alive and contact was finally established, the rescue force was

An AH-1T is serviced aboard the USS GUADALCANAL prior to entry into the Persian Gulf. An AIM-9 Sidewinder missile is mounted to the right pylon. (US Navy)

AH-1Ws of HMM-164 operate from the USS TRIPOLI off the shore of Mogadishu, Somalia during OPERATION RESTORE HOPE in 1992. (US Navy)

quickly launched, with two Cobras assigned to escort the CH-53E transports. As the rescue force neared Basher 52's position, the Cobras took the lead to search for O'Grady and provide protection. After voice contact was made with O'Grady, one AH-1W crew marked his position with a smoke grenade while the other circled the site and guided in transports for the pickup. Although small arms fire found its mark on both CH-53s during the flight out, it was decided that the Cobras would not be turned loose against the hostile fire. The flight turned toward the safety of the Adriatic and landed aboard the KEARSARGE with their passenger.

The main building of the Iranian Sasson oil platform burns after being hit by a TOW missile fired from a Marine AH-IW. The attack was part of OPERATION PRAYING MANTIS, activated after a U.S. Navy ship struck an Iranian mine during April of 1988. Cobras of HMM-167 also destroyed platforms used to harbor small attack boats. One Marine Cobra was shot down during PRAYING MANTIS. (DoD)

Global Inventory

A limited number of AH-1 Cobras found their way into the air arms of foreign governments with U.S. support treaties. In view of the Cobra's exceptional firepower, the export of AH-1 variants to nations with American interests was (and remains) closely governed by international security agreement guidelines and subsequent State Department approval.

The first Cobras to go abroad were four 1968-vintage AH-lGs which were supplied to the Spanish Naval Air Arm during 1971 as part of the Military Assistance Program (MAP). Another four were added during 1973, one of which was a direct purchase. All eight, carrying serial numbers HA.14-1 through -8, served the Escuadrille 007 at Rota and occasionally operated from the carrier DEDALO. Four were destroyed in accidents and three were returned to the U.S. in 1985 and converted to TAH-1F trainers. The final AH-1G remained in storage at Rota.

During 1979 and 1980, two AH-lEs went to Japan to fill an order by the Bell-licensed Mitsui & Company. After extensive evaluation, an agreement was signed for Japanese production of AH-1S(TOW)s by Fuji Heavy Industries, along with T53-K-703 engines to be built by Kawasaki. A total of 54 machines were produced during the late 1980s, all of which served the Japanese Ground Self Defense Force (JGSDF). A number were brought up to AH-1F standards and remain in service.

The Israeli Defense/Air Force (IDAF) received six AH-lGs during 1977, which were converted to AH-1Qs. They were followed by six AH-1Es which were eventually converted to AH-lSs. By 1985, the IDAF had acquired 30 AH-1Fs through five separate orders. A combination of the three models, totaling nearly 40 aircraft, remained in service into the 1990s for the anti-tank mission. During 1995 Israel ordered an additional 14 AH-lEs to replace the Hughes 500MD Defenders used by the IDAF school.

Before U.S. relations with Iran ceased, the country received a total of 202 AH-lJs, 140 of which were standard models. They were operated by the Imperial Iranian Army Aviation (IIAA), which assigned them serials 3-4401 through 4540. Numbers 3-4402, 4412 and 4484 were converted to AH-1J(TOW) as evaluation platforms. The remaining 62 were delivered as AH-1J(TOW) and given serials 3-4541 through 4602 The aircraft were called "International" AH-lJs, which differed from the USMC version by having Bell Model 214 "Huey Plus" components, which included an uprated engine, as well as larger main and tail rotors. Prior to the "Islamic Revolution" in 1979, all 202 AH-lJs were based at Isfahan. It's doubtful that Iran's AH-lJs, or the few captured from Iran by Iraq, remain air worthy.

Adding to the Cobra presence in the Middle East was Jordan, which ordered 24 AH-1Fs during the early 1980s. They were delivered during 1985 and assigned serials 82-24077 through 24100. During 1995, Jordan placed an order for two AH-1Ps along with two TAH-lPs. All operated from King Abdullah Air Base near Amman.

Pakistan took delivery of 20 AH-1Fs during the early 1980s, which equipped Pakistan's army.

The government of Bahrain, which has operated an undisclosed number of AH-1Fs, placed an order for six AH-1Ps and possibly as many as 26 AH-1Fs during 1995.

Cobras became a part of South Korea's large helicopter force during the late 1970s when it took delivery of eight International AH-1J(TOW)s. Korea obtained an additional 90 Cobras from April 1990 to April 1992.

Thailand received an initial batch of four AH-1Fs during the late 1970s, followed by another four during 1990. Designated HJ.ls in Royal Thai Army service, the Cobras formed the sole dedicated attack portion of the Aviation Battalion at Lop Buri.

These AH-1Gs of the Spanish Navy were the first Cobras to be exported. The four were finished in Dark Blue Gray. (Bell)

By the 1990s, the AH-1W SuperCobra exhibited worldwide appeal to nations that sought a cost effective, advanced and reliable gunship. A number of foreign governments expressed their interest in the AH-lW's survivability, high mission availability rates, low manpower requirement and adverse weather capability.

Turkey first received 24 secondhand AH-lPs from the U.S. and ordered five AH-lWs, which were sold under the U.S. Foreign Military Sales (FMS) program and delivered during 1990. Later an additional five were ordered for the Army's Attack Helicopter Battalion at Ankara. Turkey withdrew an order for an additional ten after Congress delayed approval.

A newcomer to AH-lW sales is Taiwan, which ordered 16 examples, with a follow-on order for 22. The SuperCobras equip the 1st Attack Squadron at Lungtan and the 2nd at Tainan. Another recent customer is the Philippines, which placed a Cobra order during 1996.

As part of their integration as a NATO member, the government of Romania teamed up with Bell during mid 1995 to propose the production of 96 AH-1Fs. The intent of the agreement was to establish commonality with NATO forces within the guidelines of the Central Forces Europe Treaty. The AH-1Fs are to be produced in Romania with delivery scheduled between 1999 and 2005. Romania's intent to alter the proposal one year later, in favor of AH-lWs, elicited State Department warnings that approval would be more difficult to obtain in view of technology-transfer issues.

In May 1992, Bell and the British firm GEC Marconi announced plans to jointly produce an AH-lW variant called the "Venom." Intended to fulfill the British Army's attack helicopter requirement, the Cobra Venom was to combine a GEC's advanced technology cockpit with the AH-lW airframe for superior performance and cost effectiveness. However, the project lost to the AH-64 since the British Army had its sights set on the Apache, and Bell/GEC had yet to present a flying prototype.

Number 4402 was delivered to Iran as an AH-1J and was the first to be converted to TOW configuration. The TOW missile launchers and rotor blades were included in the tan and brown camouflage. (Robert F. Dorr via Nick Williams)

The first AH-1S(TOW) built under license by Fuji fires 2.75-inch rockets from a launcher mounted inboard of the TOW launcher. (Bell)

One of 20 AH-1Fs which went to the Pakistani Army during the 1980s. (Bell)

The first of eight AH-1J(TOW)s delivered to South Korea. (Bell)

Turkish AH-1Ws are destined to become a rare sight since Turkey canceled orders for additional machines when the U.S. Congress continually stalled approval of the sales. (Bell)

One of eight AH-1Fs which formed the Royal Thai Army's attack helicopter fleet. (Bell)

Flying without gunners, a trio of AH-1Fs are being test flown prior to delivery to Jordan's Air Force. (Bell)

Bell artists applied Chinese markings to this AH-IW in anticipation of sales to Taiwan. (Bell)

47

Special Projects

Considering the number of Cobras produced, the scope of their development and widespread use, it's not surprising that some played an important part in various test programs. A number of Cobras were also participants in special programs carried out by non-military agencies.

At least three AH-lGs are known to have been converted to test beds for various systems such as the Hellfire missile. Labeled a JAH-1G, (71-20985) was used to evaluate an experimental GE M197 20mm cannon capable of twice its normal 750 rpm rate of fire. An associated Bell stabilized optical sight and a Hughes laser range finder were mounted in the Cobra's nose.

During 1984, Bell developed a highly modified Cobra for research of Advanced Rotorcraft Technology Integration (ARTI). The test aircraft, designated YAH-lS (Bell's Model 249), was initially used to test the Model 412 four-bladed main rotor and the Advanced Capability (ADCAP) concept. It was then put to use as a test platform for the Army's Light Helicopter Experimental (LHX) program. During 1986, the ARTI program embodied a single pilot cockpit which reduced the pilot's workload for the Scout/Attack (SCAT) LHX. For that series of tests, Bell teamed up with Honeywell to develop an advanced digital flight control system. The concept centered around a sophisticated electronics array that allowed hands-off during the full flight envelope, including hovering, which freed the pilot for other tasks.

An important adjunct in the Cobra's history was Bell's entry into the U.S. Army's Advanced Attack Helicopter (AAH) Task Force, established during November 1972, following the forced cancellation of the AH-56 Cheyenne program. Its goal was to find high performance aircraft able to operate day or night, in adverse weather, strike with extreme accuracy and survive extensive battle damage.

Bell attempted to fill the tall order with its Model 409, designated YAH-63, which was one of two designs selected in June 1973. Its competitor was the Hughes Model 77, which the Army designated YAH-64. Two YAH-63 flying prototypes and a ground mock-up were built, which featured wheeled gear and a flat plate canopy over the familiar tandem cockpit, where the YAH-63 pilot was positioned in front for better NOE operation. Based on the Model 309 KingCobra, the YAH-63 was powered by a pair of 1,536shp GE T700-GE-700 engines, the same as those specified for the YAH-64. The aircraft's maximum gross weight was 15,000 pounds and had a maximum speed of 200 mph. Like the Cobra, the YAH-63 featured the characteristic two-bladed, wide-chord main rotor and carried its ordnance on stub wings. A three-barreled 30mm cannon was mounted in a chin turret.

The first prototype (73-22246) made its maiden flight on 1 October 1975. It was repaired after a crash the following June in time to participate along with the second prototype (73-22247) in an Army "fly-off" against the YAH-64. The Hughes design was selected for the AAH program on 10 December 1976. Though similar in appearance, the larger and heavier YAH-64 prototype featured a four-bladed main and tail rotor, as well as a tail wheel, compared to the YAH-63's nose wheel.

During September 1981, one AH-1G (66-15345) and two AH-lSs (69-16430 and 71-20983) were acquired by the U.S. Navy's Test Pilot School at NAS Patuxent River for evaluations.

The U.S. Army Aeroflightdynamics Directorate and NASA have had three Cobras for research projects. AH-1G serial number 66-15248 (the first production Cobra) went from the Army's maintenance depot at Corpus Christi to NASA's Langley Research Center in December 1972 for acoustics phenomena study and rotor aerodynamics and performance research. It was transferred to the Ames Research Center at Moffett Field, California in March 1978, where it served as a chase aircraft before it was returned to the Army in 1983.

Bell's entry in the Army's AAH competition, held during the 1970s, was the YAH-63. Intended as the Cobra's eventual replacement, the YAH-63 featured a distinctive T-tail. (Bell)

During May 1985, the Ames facility acquired a JAH-1S (77-22768) which was originally an AH-lE. In NASA service, it bore the registration N73ONA. During November 1987, Ames obtained a TH-1S from Ft Rucker, where it saw use as a surrogate trainer for AH-64 pilots. Serial number 70-15979, a Vietnam veteran, is presently designated an NAH-lS as a test bed for a wide variety of research programs, including evaluation of new design guidelines for the presentation of graphics data on helmet-mounted displays. Other studies involve voice computers and headset noise level reductions. Like its predecessor, the NAH-1S was given registration N736NA.

Among other modified Cobras which had their service careers extended, were those operated by the U.S. Customs Service. The USCS is known to have used four, and possibly as many as eight, Cobras from 1980 to 1985 for drug interdiction. These were but a few machines sanctioned for use by non-military forces. The nose turrets of U.S. Customs Service AH-1s were replaced by powerful "Nitesun" searchlights.

The Army Cobra's replacement during the AAH competition; the Army assigned both YAH-64 prototypes serial numbers consecutive with those of the YAH-63s. Alongside is Bell's competitor during evaluation of both types. (MAP)

The crew of the Model 249 demonstrate the hands-off hovering capability made possible by a sophisticated electronics suite. (Bell)

Included among the wide variety of weapons systems evaluated on the Model 249 was the Hellfire missile, initially developed for the Army's Apache. (Bell)

Bell's Model 249, also called the Cobra 2000, flew with the four-blade 412 rotor system. (Bell)

An AH-1G, fitted with an early IR exhaust suppressor, assigned to NASA's Ames Research Center. (NASA)

1083 Mi-24 Hind

1133 H-60 Blackhawk

MORE
HELICOPTERS
From
squadron/signal publications

1146 H-34 Choctaw

1150 H-3 Sea King